THE BLINDNESS CURE

Master Deac

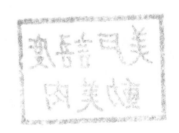

CAROL E. MCMAHON, PH.D.
WITH MASTER DEAC CATALDO

THE BLINDNESS CURE
HOW TO RESTORE AWARENESS
AND WHY YOU NEED TO

2008

THE BLINDNESS CURE

THE BLINDNESS CURE

To B. R. B.

PREFACE

I never saw your face. I do not know your name. This book however, was written for you. Throughout years of writing, I imagined you reading. I knew a moment would come when you see the light, and know that you have the answer and that you need never be helpless again. I remembered the joy I felt when I had this realization, and the prospect of your joy kept me going. I thank you for giving my life such purpose.

My thanks go too to those who helped in tangible ways, kind readers of early drafts who urged me on: Fran Majeski, Terry and Bob Cyr, Josh Clayson, Pat Daigeler, Ada Kanu, Carolyn Lee, Malinda Lounsbury; Amy Tillinghast; Mary K. Mogavero; Ellen Mogavero; Ann Katherine Mogavero; Robert Garra; Roberta Burns and Monica Parikh.

Editor and infinitely patient human Margo Rideout gave me unthinkably gentle correction.

Playwright, friend and comedic genius Ken Friedman raised my spirits and through his natural skepticism, forced me into greater clarity.

Marge Hudak supported me with trust, love and wisdom; Rae Ann Shelly with a generous heart and wisdom beyond her years.

True healers Dr. Michael Wilson and Wendy Orlowski, Dr. Mahendra Mirani, and Certified Rolfer Gary Robb, kept me well.

Sweet Adelines Chorus Directors Sue Gentile and Sonny Durphy provided the posture exercises in the how-to sections.

My good neighbors the Foleys lent me their ten-acre woods where my soul was restored.

Toward the end of writing, in need of inspiration and friendship, I found it in Spraguebrook, a beautifully kept County Park near my home. I am indebted for this to the staff: Michael Collins; Walter Cork; Frank Douglas Domster; Michael Domster; John Garner and James Maiarana.

Carolyn Trinkley and Sue Roush sang with me and the bond of friendship helped carry me through.

My husband, Dr. Raj Parikh, knew as I did that this book *had to be* written. He too devoted his life to it through his devotion to me. He was a one-man granting foundation, supporting me unfalteringly in financial, and in technical and moral support. No one on earth could have taken his place. No one ever will.

Lastly and lovingly, I want to thank my daughter who served as my Zen Master from 1978 to 1981.

CHAPTER ONE
A BREAKTHROUGH; A NEW TOOL;
A GUARANTEE

Anything we do can be done better.

Franz Theodore Stone III, Former
President, Columbus McKinnon Chain

This book shows you how to restore awareness. Most of us do not know we need to. A demonstration proves we do.

Look at the face of a clock. The minute hand is moving. The hour hand is too. Can you see them move?

Straining to see does not help. Our eyes are not to blame. Low awareness is. It takes very little awareness to see the fast movement of the second hand. It takes deeper awareness to see the slower hands move, and this we lack. If full awareness is one hundred percent, we might have as little as five percent on average. Even when we think we are aware, *we cannot see what is before our eyes.*

This is the "blindness" referred to in the title, the blindness this book cures. We need the cure because without awareness our eyes are not open to beauty, our senses are not open to pleasure, our minds are not open to truth and our hearts are not open to love. Low awareness keeps us from happiness.

These chapters offer a solution in the form of a new, efficient way to restore awareness. It is the Feedback Method.

The Feedback Method

The new method is a form of meditation, but it has something other methods lack. It has "feedback." Let me explain the vital difference feedback makes.

- Meditation: What's Missing?

I once read of a man in England who meditated faithfully for most of his life. When a meditation Master came to town, this man approached him. He said that after meditating for twenty years he was no better off than when he began. He was still burdened by the same problems. You can meditate faithfully and accomplish very little. Indeed thousands of years of meditation have made enlightenment no less rare, no less mysterious.

Despite its shortfall, meditation has always been done in much the same way. A spiritual practice by tradition, meditation is not subject to criticism. I took a critical, scientific approach however, and I found that meditation is missing something. Let me show you what I discovered.

I graduated in psychology from Penn State in the heyday Transcendental Meditation (TM). Its claim of a "cure for mental illness" caught my attention. "Perfect mental balance," was promised, "a balance of mind never upset by any event under the canopy of heaven (Narayananda, page 78)." I went to learn TM skeptical and was amazed at the powerful, positive change that occurred in me. I sensed that the lofty claims might somehow be justified.

In time however I saw that the method failed to fulfill its promise. Most students gained only rest and relaxation. Some did not benefit at all. I had great success with TM but only at first. In a few months I found I could recite a mantra and worry about something at the same time. The method was unreliable, but the potential I had seen drew me to meditation. A wise man had taught me that anything we do can be done better. Applying this I set out to find a reliable, efficient way to meditate. First I had to find out what made meditation work. I had to isolate its active ingredient. This turned out to be easy.

The Active Ingredient?

Over-viewing meditation methods, I found many forms. Some sat still, some moved, some were vocal, some silent. All however had one thing in common. Each *attended to* something (a mantra or the breath, for instance). Attention and only attention was present in all. By process of elimination, attention proved to be the active ingredient. In other words, it was not the sitting, the mantra or the chant that made meditation work.

Attention stills the restless mind. With it meditation moves mountains. Without it we while away our time.

Knowing attention was the key to success, I saw that meditation was missing something. It lacks a way to harness attention. "You sit down to meditate," said meditation teacher Roger Walsh, "and ten minutes later you wake up and realize you are not on the beach in Hawaii." You set out to concentrate but you lose attention and end up drifting, dreaming or dozing off. Attention is easily lost because it slips away unseen. Indeed, we lose attention without knowing we are losing it.

I knew now what meditation was missing. It needed a way to monitor attention. An efficient method would *confirm* attention. It would tell you when you are on target and alert you when you wander off. Psychology has a word for what was needed: "feedback."

Without feedback, meditation is like shooting darts blindfolded. Your target is attention, but if you cannot see your target you cannot correct your aim. Feedback lets you see what you are doing and feedback is necessary for learning any skill, including attending. Without feedback meditation is license to drift and dream.

Looking for Feedback

Knowing what was needed, I searched the traditions for a feedback-based method. I found rich stores of wisdom and countless methods (there are more than two hundred in India alone). All however lacked confirmation of attention, the feedback necessary for learning.

"There are no special techniques," wrote a Buddhist Master, "just watch the tip of your nose for six hours in the daytime and six hours at night (in Cleary, 1978, page 50)." Without feedback, meditation instruction tended to be as nebulous as the experience itself. I stopped searching and tried to devise a new method. For months I taxed my brain but found no better way. I was discouraged enough to give up when by accident I found the answer.

-    The Answer

I was exploring an open-eyed method, the "open gaze" of Zen practice. One day meditating, the afternoon sun through a picture window cast vivid shadows in the ridges of my sculpted carpet. A dark spot the size of a pea caught my eye. I wondered...Could a spot serve as an anchor for attention? I zeroed in and within seconds, my search for efficient meditation ended.

It ended when a small halo of light appeared around the spot when I focused attention.

What caused the light?

My attention did. Attention held my eyes still. This held the image in the same place on my eyes' retinas. Photo-pigment was used up (like exposed photographic film). This created visual distortion in the form of light.

As long as I focused attention I saw this halo of light. When my mind wandered however, my eyes wandered and the light disappeared. The light confirmed attention. I could now see what I was doing. I could attend to attention, mind my mind. The spot on the floor could not anchor attention. The distortion however could. It was feedback. It let me take charge. Within an hour I had the breakthrough meditation seeks, the breakthrough to full awareness that is known as enlightenment. From that moment I knew the purpose of my life was to show you how to do the same. This book does that.

Now let me explain the advantages of the Feedback Method.

Advantages of the Feedback Method

Attention deficit is everyone's problem. Low awareness is the human condition. Famed psychologist William James noted that we can voluntarily sustain attention for only a few seconds. Feedback changes this. Holding on to feedback you can sustain attention indefinitely. You can hold on to attention the way you can grab a rope for a tow. You can let it convey you straight to awareness. You can then "see the light" literally and figuratively.

The method is simple and easy to use. As pictured in Figure 1 (Chapter Six, page 72) a disc with a bull's eye is placed on the floor. Attention is your target. Feedback (light or other distortion) means a direct hit. There is nothing nebulous here and no guesswork involved. Either you have feedback or you do not. You simply sit and watch the show your attention is producing. Consider the advantages of feedback.

ADVANTAGES OF FEEDBACK	
With Feedback	**Without Feedback**
"No guesswork" instructions	Nebulous instructions
Unproductive practice time can be avoided	Unproductive practice time likely
Easy to hold attention	Hard to hold attention for more than a few seconds
Fast practice skill development	Slow (or even no) practice skill development
Energized relaxation	Collapsed relaxation likely
Guaranteed success	No guarantee possible

- <u>Advantages of Feedback</u>

• <u>Practice Skill Develops Fast.</u>

Traditional meditation is like shooting darts blindfold. If you cannot correct your aim, your skill is not likely to improve with practice. You might even get *less* effective over time. (I did with TM.)

A Zen Master said: "After twenty years you can finally say you have begun to learn how to sit…Many will take even longer." Feedback changes this. Seeing what you are doing you get better automatically. Just doing it your skill improves, and great gains come from doing it *better*, not necessarily longer. With feedback five minutes of practice has a visible payoff. Without feedback you might sit for hours (or possibly years like the man in England), with little apparent benefit.

• <u>Progress Takes Less Time.</u>

Buddhist tradition says: "Just sit…and eventually, maybe after many lifetimes, you will come upon the truth." This assumes many lifetimes of drifting and dreaming.

Feedback changes this. A butterfly mind takes a bee-line. Unproductive practice time is avoidable. Quality, not quantity of practice counts most here, not hours spent meditating, but *minutes on target*. Beginners have instant success, and as skill advances less time is needed to bring greater benefit.

Feedback is to meditation what good steering is to navigation. Traditional meditation wanders, "visiting realms," ranging into fantasy. Feedback prevents wandering, and when you do not wander you cover ground fast. This is straight-line meditation, the shortest distance between where you are now and where you want to be. Now you can guide yourself straight to the goal.

- You Can Guide Yourself.

Meditation students are often taught there is no right or wrong way to do it. They sit passively, hoping for luck.

Why is meditation so passive? Because it has to be. Being aggressive would be like running full speed when you are not sure where you are going.

With the feedback method you can see where you are going and feedback corrects your course. This makes feedback an ideal meditation teacher.

Shooting darts blindfolded is the wrong way to practice darts. Meditation without feedback is similarly inefficient. With feedback you *can* run full speed to your goal.

- You Can Go for the Goal.

You can tell if someone is driving blind. He is all over the road. Inconsistent results of meditation show the same directional instability. It is all too easy to meditate in circles.

Some meditation teachers encourage students by saying there is no goal. Some even say there is nothing to be gained, but this puts a damper on motivation to practice. Who wants to work toward no goal?

The new method takes care of this too. There *is* a goal. It is awareness. Feedback brings it in easy reach. You can aim high.

- You Can Aim High.

Many meditate for relaxation, but meditating for relaxation is like attending a banquet and eating crumbs off the floor. With feedback you feast at the banquet. Traditional meditation gets you into the banquet hall, but feedback sits you down at the table to feast. You can aim higher and you can count on success.

- Success is Guaranteed.

Meditation is a trial and error process but with traditional meditation, most error goes undetected. Without confirmed attention there is no guarantee of success.

With the Feedback Method, success follows a simple formula: *Feedback means attention. Attention means success.* That is why with feedback, success is guaranteed.

How to Use this Book

Awareness is a spacious mansion filled with riches. It is yours from birth.

The thinking mind is a noisy trouble making tenant.

This tenant has taken over and shut you out. With this book you can reclaim your mansion. Awareness can be restored.

In a sense we are meant to function aware the way a car is designed to run on gas. Only running on gas does the engine function right. When aware, we run smoothly on all cylinders with eyes open to beauty; senses open to pleasure; minds open to truth and hearts to love. Enlightenment is nothing apart from such awareness. I hope that with this book enlightenment will become less mysterious and less rare.

We thought no "recipe" or simple guide to enlightenment was possible. Thanks to feedback, this is no longer true. Use this book as you would a recipe. Take each step in sequence, adding what you need (motivation; Self-tests, etc.) when you need it.

• The How-to Chapters

They say when you are ready the teacher will appear. Look in the mirror and behold your guide. Self-guidance is complete here: feedback guides your practice and Self-tests guide your progress.

Awareness is uncharted territory. You need Self-tests to know where you stand. Nearly two hundred are provided here. They will confirm your progress and tell you when to move on.

The exercises taught here (beginner, intermediate and advanced) offer three ways to get where you need to go. They are like the three ways to go gate to gate in a large airport. You can walk, use the ramp, or take the rapid rail. Walking is slowest. The moving ramp is faster, and the rapid rail is faster still. The first option is like Exercise One (Chapter Two), a beginner's orientation. This exercise walks. No feedback is involved and like traditional meditation, it wanders off course easily. Feedback is introduced in the basic exercise in Chapter Six (*The Feedback*

Method). This more efficient exercise, like a moving ramp, takes you in a straight line so you can not lose your way. *Advanced Practice* (Chapter Ten) is the rapid rail. It conveys you straight to full awareness and the enlightenment breakthrough (Chapter Eleven, *Breakthrough!*).

- The Narrative Chapters

The Feedback Method is a power tool that sharpens with use until it cuts through everything. Chapters Three, Four and Five: *"Original Perfection:" A Baby's Awareness; Confusion and Illusion: How Concepts Blind Us,* and *Self-interest and the Illusion of Love* explain what you can gain with the instruction in this book.

A bright source of wisdom lights our way here. It is the martial tradition: Karate dō (The Way of the Empty Hand). It came to be included here by mysterious means.

Several years ago, when work on the book was nearing completion, unlikely events led me to a Karate studio. There I met Master Deac Cataldo, tenth degree black belt and Sixth Master of Karate dō. Master Deac said: "You know it is destiny that we meet." Strangely I did know though I had no idea why this meeting was destined.

I stayed. I became a student, and the tradition's wisdom was passed to me. It came in face-to-face teachings as it had passed through four and a half centuries from Master Darama through Master SiFu, Master TiLe, Master MoKow and from Master Choe to Master Deac. Its main message: *awareness is everything.* The words plugged into my manuscript like charged wires.

Training in Karate dō involves transfer of power from teacher to student. Master Choe told Master Deac: "The power of my mind transfers to you, becoming the power of your mind." My teacher's power is legendary. You will feel it in these pages.

- Motivation Chapters

The balance of the book helps you keep going strong. Chapter Seven (*How to Use and Prevent Pain*) explains the role pain can play as guidance. Chapter Eight (*Trouble-Shooting*) helps solve problems that interfere with practice. A separate chapter (Nine) treats *How to Stay Motivated,* and the final chapters offer inspiration.

Master Choe taught: "We are containers but we have no idea how large we are and we are nowhere near full." The final chapters show you how large you are. They are Chapter Twelve, *Facets of the Jewel*, Chapter Thirteen, *How to See God,* and Chapter Fourteen, *Being Love.* You can find inspiration here and this will help because motivation is all-important. If it is good, outcome is good and if it is great, as Zen puts it: "You will astonish heaven and shake the earth." Feedback guarantees it.

-    <u>Starting In</u>

Much here is new and surprising, but nothing is complicated. Start in with a lesson of simplicity. This could even be called a one-step program. Attention restores awareness. Awareness is all you need.

I will speak directly to you, not as a psychologist but as one human being to another. At the deepest level you and I are the same. I found my mansion of awareness and I can guide you to yours. A lifetime will not exhaust all you can gain from this book.

Start wherever you are. It does not matter if you are in a high stress job, a hospital bed or a prison cell. Your Mansion is not in the mountains of Tibet. It is right before your eyes.

Entry here is a pivotal life step. Think of it this way: your whole life has led to this moment; holding this book; breathing this breath, reading this sentence. Know that at this moment your destiny is in your hands.

CHAPTER TWO
A BEGINNER EXERCISE

It is all awareness! Awareness! Awareness!
Master Deac

If you are new to meditation, start here with this beginner level TM type exercise. If you are an experienced meditator, start with the Feedback Method in Chapter Six, but review this chapter and take the Self-tests to see where you stand.

An Indian fable tells of a ferry crossing where one passenger was a learned priest, all too proud of his scholarship. As they traveled he boasted on and on.

All aboard admired and praised him, except for one young man who remained silent. This irritated the priest.

"Do you know the Scriptures?" he asked the young man.

"No reverend sir," he answered.

"Do you know the ancient writings?"

"No reverend sir," the young man replied.

"Do you know any philosophy whatsoever?"

"No reverend sir," he said again.

They traveled on, the scholar preaching in the same vain manner when suddenly the ferry sprung a leak. Everyone aboard knew they would not reach the shore.

Now the young man spoke. "Sir, can you swim?"

"No" answered the scholar.

"I know no philosophy but I can swim," the young man said.

Throughout these chapters, we are here not to analyze but to act. This is a path of action, not words.

Are you ready?

Take the plunge.

Exercise One: A Beginners' Orientation

Attention stills the wandering mind. In the silence that follows, awareness dawns. With awareness comes a "relaxation response" (Benson, 1975) that may surprise you. Spend a week with this exercise. It will give you a sense of where you are going and how you will get there. First pick the right time and place for practice.

- ### The Right Time

How much time you spend is up to you. More time brings more benefit. A half hour daily is recommended. Put in no less than fifteen minutes.

Not just any half hour will do. Make it *prime time*: a wide-awake, energetic time when you could do anything well. It should not be right after eating or right after waking up. You may feel wide-awake in the morning, but brain waves show signs of sleep for some time after waking.

No one time is right for everyone. Morning people are energetic early, night people later. Do not hesitate to practice late if it works for you.

Now find the right place.

- ### The Right Place

Your setting should be private and quiet. Arrange not to be disturbed. Loosen tight clothing. Lie on a firm bed, mat or carpet. Use no pillow or blanket. If you can not lie down without dozing, sit as illustrated in Figure 1 (page 72). Now close your eyes and direct attention inward. You are ready to begin.

- ### Focus on "A"

In this exercise you will focus on a sound. Repeat "A" silently at a steady pace. Aim to *fill* your mind, not empty it. Fill your mind with "A."

If you find yourself planning your day or wondering what to have for dinner, simply return to "A." If distracted, come back to "A." Attention to "A" is what you are here for. Come back again and again.

- ### Just Let it Happen

Think of yourself as a juggler. Your thoughts are balls kept in motion by constant thinking. Normally you juggle all the time. Stop juggling however and the balls come to rest, settled by a sort of "inner gravity."

How do you stop juggling? By doing something else instead. Here you attend to "A" and just let it happen.

- "Pops and Tingles"

As thoughts settle, knots of tension untie. A student called the feelings "pops and tingles:"

- tingling fingers or toes
- quivering muscles
- heavy or light body
- watering eyes
- increased saliva
- clearing of sinuses
- warm hands or feet
- deeper, slower breathing
- arm or leg jerks

Do not dwell on sensations like these but hear what they have to say: you are getting the job done.

Now for some dos and don'ts.

Dos and Don'ts

- Do Stay Alert. Be alert. Even lying down, stay on your toes!
- Don't Forget What You Are Here For. Remember you are here for one thing only: not to quiet mind, not to relax, not even to build awareness. Only attend to "A". Just "A."
- Don't Try, Just Do It. Trying gets in the way. Just do it.

- Ending the Exercise

It takes time to get into this. The first half of a session is less effective than the last. Stay the whole time.

End your exercise with a timer or clock placed where easily seen. Get up slowly and ease back into your routine.

Do this daily for one week (longer if you like). You will know when to move on: when it's right it feels right.

Problem File: Questions and Answers

Here are answers to some common questions. They may match your own.

Having Doubts?

In Islamic folklore, a Prince had to answer several questions before he could be King. One was "What is the greatest thing (in the sense of size) that exists?" He answered correctly: "The greatest thing is *doubt* (Owadally, 2003, page 32)."

Everyone has doubts. You may doubt that this technique will work for you.

Let me share a lesson I learned from a student we will call Paul. He was forty-five, twice divorced and struggling with alcoholism. He wanted to talk, but time ran short and I asked him to move to the instruments. Heart rate, skin conductance and like measures would monitor his practice. I took baseline readings and asked him to close his eyes and repeat "A."

I watched and waited. Three minutes passed and the instruments showed no change. Paul had tense muscles, a rapid pulse and cold hands. There was plenty of room for improvement, yet no change. I usually saw change within seconds, but five minutes passed with none. In the dim light I searched his face for an explanation. I saw no confusion or strain. I tried encouragement: "We will be just a few minutes more. Remember, stay with 'A' and just let it happen."

Another five minutes passed with no change. What could be wrong? What would I tell him? Finally I said: "I'm sorry but it didn't work."

He sat still and silent a moment. Then he turned to me and said: "I didn't do what you told me to do."

I learned an important lesson from this. I was wrong to say: "*It* didn't work." Paul had not worked. He had the power. "*It*" has none.

If you have doubts, if you find yourself saying: "It won't work," or "It did not work for me today," remember Paul's lesson. There is no "it." Your not attending is the only way to fail.

Words Instead of "A?"

Meditation sometimes uses meaningful words like "love" and "peace." Can words be used instead of "A?"

14

It's best to stick with "A." Its energetic quality goes with attention, and more important, it has no meaning. Use "A" to help anchor attention. Meaningful words set you sailing away.

Tapes Instead?

Meditation tapes are available. Can they substitute for this?

Tapes can not substitute for this exercise. Let me explain why.

Years ago, so-called "reducing machines" were popular. They passively moved the limbs, lifting legs and arms while reducers rested. They were not popular for long because they were not effective. You have to work to tone muscle. The same goes for building awareness. A voice on a tape can relax you, but building awareness takes focused attention. As in the gym, you have to work out.

Can You Add Music?

Can you add music?

Nothing can be added to this without taking away from it. Do not add music, nature sounds or incense. The goal is *undivided* attention. Just attend to "A."

What to Expect from a Session?

What can you expect from a practice session?

Experience ranges from feeling nothing to feeling totally different. Expect thoughts to flow more like a gentle brook than like the great gorge rapids; to soothe rather than distress you. If you were worried, you will be less worried after a session. If you were angry, you will be less angry. Whatever is going on in your life, you will be more accepting because of the understanding that comes with awareness.

Expect this but do not look for results. Pessimists will be discouraged. Optimists will think they are already done. Just watch results unfold. Ben Franklin said: "He that can have patience can have what he will."

Can You Bring it on with Words?

I have been asked: "What should I say to myself to bring this on in the course of the day?" This is like a weight lifter asking: "What can I say to myself to build muscle?"

Attention is pumping iron. Awareness is the muscle it builds. Nothing you can say helps. Even trying to be mindful can interfere if the trying is mental noise. Count on awareness to build automatically with attention.

Trying to Relax?

Awareness chauffeurs you to relaxation. Trying only gets in the way.

Scientists at the Medical College of Georgia studied effects of TM on blood pressure. They were surprised when a control group of non-meditators, told simply to relax, showed increased vascular constriction and higher blood pressure (*Men's Journal*, March 2000, page 70). I saw the same effect on measures I monitored. If I saw tension increase and asked: "Are you trying to relax," often the answer was: "Yes."

Trying divides attention and drains energy. Do not try to relax. This is like floating. Trying to float makes you sink. Just let go and float on "A."

A Sleep Aid?

If you have trouble sleeping you may be tempted to use this, but falling asleep even once can lead to a drowsy practice habit. Do the exercise before bed if you like, but finish, emerge and then fall asleep naturally.

Taking Medication?

I heard that people who meditate see doctors forty-three percent less than those who do not. Meditation affects the body in many healthful ways. If you are taking medication, tell your doctor what you are doing. In some cases a dosage adjustment or even discontinuation might be advised.

No More "Pops and Tingles?"

Have the pops and tingles stopped?

This is not a problem but a good sign. Pops and tingles diminish as you go. When all knots of tension are untied, they stop completely.

Are You Finished?

Do you "feel like your old self again?"

If so, ask yourself this: Who got you into trouble in the first place?

The Feedback Method lets you aim higher. Why stop short? If you feel like your old self again you are not finished. You have just begun.

Beginner Self-tests

Thirty-one beginner Self-tests are offered here. Some test dawning awareness. Others measure what Jon Kabat-Zinn (2005) calls "dis-ease," the stress and tension that come as harmful effects of low awareness. Ration these Self-tests. Take a few now, and return for more later.

Self-test 1: Find Your 'SQ.'

The Sanity Quotient (SQ) questionnaire is an index of stress and tension. Take it now and later for before-and-after comparison.

Put a check in one column at the right of each item. Answer all twenty-five. (If your answer is almost always, check "Always." If it is almost never check "Never.") Your score is for you alone to see, so give frank answers.

THE 'SQ' TEST

To find your 'SQ', check the column that best describes you:
1 - Sometimes; 2 - Always; 3 - Never

		1 Sometimes	2 Always	3 Never
1	I talk to myself silently, continuously throughout the day			
2	My head, neck or back aches from tension..........................			
3	I awaken feeling tires and not refreshed..........................			
4	It is difficult for me to forgive and forget..........................			
5	I feel uncomfortable when people talk very slowly			
6	I catch myself with my teeth clenched			
7	I suspect that others are happier and better adjusted than I am			
8	My hands are cold, even in a warm room			
9	I feel alone and isolated			
10	I find relief in daydreams and fantasies			
11	I rehearse imaginary conversations of what I should have said, but didn't			
12	I am kept awake by a racing mind			
13	I use antacids or laxatives			
14	I feel a strong craving for happiness and the good things in life			
15	I feel lighthearted or dizzy without any apparent physical cause.................			
16	When silence comes over a room I feel uncomfortable			
17	I drink alcohol or take drugs to help me relax			
18	I find myself powerless to stop an advertising jingle or song that is playing in my head			
19	I interpret unusual sensations in my body as symptoms of disease			
20	Waiting in lines at the bank or store causes me anxiety			
21	My heart beats rapidly, even though I am not exercising			
22	Fear keeps me from doing things I would like to do			
23	I am worried or pessimistic about my future			
24	While working, I am in a hurry to get to the next thing			
25	I fear that I may lose control			

YOUR 'SQ' TEST SCORE

To find your score:

Total the number of checks in column one and column two

	Sometimes' total	Always' total
Put the totals in Box a and Box b	Box a	Box b

Multiply the number in Box b by 4 — Box b x 4 = Box c

Add the number in Box a to the number in Box c — Box a + Box c = Box d

Subtract the number in Box d from 100 — 100 - Box d =

The Remainder is your 'SQ'

To see how your score compares:
-0 to 69 is below average score
-70 to 80 is average
-81-90 is above average
-91-100 is well above average

Find Your Score

When finished, count the checks in each column. Plug in the "Sometimes" and "Always" column totals as directed. Figure up your score.

What Your Score Means

Low scores are normal for beginners. As awareness grows however, Sanity Quotients rise. Even perfect scores (100) are possible. Save your results. We will return to them later.

Tests of Tension

Thinking activates the body. Ills we attribute to "stress" reflect this activation. As soon as you start your exercise mental noise and activation start to decline. Muscles relax; oxygen-need lowers; heart rate slows; hands warm, etc., as body comes into balance. Improvement in stress-ravaged health follows. Headaches are less frequent and less severe; tension-related pain eases; elevated blood pressure goes down. Secondary gains like better sleep and increased energy are also standard. Books on health effects of meditation are available (*The Relaxation Response*, Benson, 1975; *Meditation as Medicine*, Khalsa & Stauth, 2002) if you want to learn more.

Self-tests 2, 3, 4 and 5 measure bodily changes.

Self-test 2: The Paper Test.

Do you have a steady hand? Test and see.

Before your exercise, extend an arm, palm down, fingers apart. Place a sheet of paper on the back of your hand extending beyond your fingertips. Vibration at the edges of the sheet indicates a fine tremor.

Try it again after your exercise. Tremor may be gone.

Self-test 3: Minute to Minute Tension.

Answer yes or no.
1. Are you rushing to finish this so you can go on to something else?
2. Is your jaw clenched?
3. Are your shoulders raised instead of resting low?
4. Are your hands cold?
5. Is your grasp of the book tighter than necessary to keep it from falling?

"Yeses" mean tension. Work toward five "nos."

Self-test 4: Before and After—Finger Temperature.

Before your session, place your fingertips in your armpit. Are they cold? After your session check again for a difference? Warmth means relaxation.

Self-test 5: Before and After—Blood Pressure.

If you have a home blood pressure instrument, check before and after readings. If your pressure is high you will probably see a decrease. Later decrease in average pressure may occur.

Self-test 6: Changes in Sleep?

You may see a change in the amount of sleep you need. Some people sleep more at first; others less. Deeper sleep is common. Do you notice change in sleep?

Self-test 7: Inner Silence?

Do you have inner silence?

Some people will start in here thinking they do. They simply have not noticed the noise.

Comedian W. C. Fields said there was a time when "drunkenness was so common it was unnoticed." Something like this might apply to the noise in our heads. Meditation teacher Jon Kabat-Zinn says people are surprised to discover their minds are "bubbling vats." If you think you have silence, keep going and be surprised.

Self-test 8: Telltale Signs?

Have you driven past your exit without seeing it?

Has someone said: "I just told you that!" when you heard nothing?

Have you missed a weather report even though you were right there?

We are lost in thought without knowing we are lost, blind without knowing we cannot see. Watch for telltale signs of low awareness.

Self-test 10: Do You Hear Pages Turning?

When his disciple did not absorb a lesson, Master Choe said: "Deacsan, you think louder than I speak." How "loud" is your thinking?

A young man stopped as he left my office, zipped his jacket and smiled. He told me he had worn that jacket for three years and had *never* heard the zipper. Now he heard it every time.

Have you heard a zipper or other new sounds? These sounds are not important in themselves. They reveal however, dawning awareness. An empty container is starting to fill. You are coming to life.

Do you hear pages turning? Read on and see what you hear.

Self-test 11: A Mind Check.

Some day at home, check your mind. Set an alarm to go off at odd times. When it sounds, notice your thoughts. Are they fast paced, negative or stressful? Are they re-runs? Are they needless energy drains?

After your practice, check your mind again for contrast.

Self-test 12: What *Really* Troubles You?

Sit back, close your eyes and bring to mind something that bothers you. It could be something someone said, or some circumstance.

Now look deeper. Is your distress caused by the circumstance, or is it caused by *your response* to it?

Your thinking causes distress. Awareness ends this. You understand yourself and others and acceptance follows. Brother Lawrence said: "Our thoughts spoil everything. All the trouble begins with them." When you know your thinking causes your troubles, you are aware.

Self-test 13: Are You Talking Less?

A woman I taught went to the same hairdresser for years. One day her hairdresser asked: "What's going on? You always talk non-stop. Now you don't say a word!"

This is an extreme case but you will probably notice such change in yourself. Constant talk is a mental noise overflow. The wise mother of a friend of mine told her son:

A still tongue makes for a wise head. The empty barrel always rattles loudest.

Rattling on in our heads drowns out everything, muting senses to the point of barely feeling alive. Thinking keeps us empty. Being less compelled to talk is a good sign.

Self-test 14: Accident Prone?

If a carpenter always carries his tools his hands are not free to function. Words are communication tools but we never put them down. Tied up mentally, awareness barely functions. Accident-proneness is one consequence. We might collide with another car, walk into a door, trip over the carpet or stub a toe on a chair right before our eyes.

As awareness grows, fewer such accidents happen.

Self-test 15: An Energy Boost?

Are you feeing drained?

Continuous thinking is our habit. Wayne Dyer cites an estimate of 60,000 thoughts a day, noting that "we have the same 60,000 thoughts today as we had yesterday (*Inspiration*, 2006, page 219)." This is like keeping your car running when you are not going anyplace. All it does is drain energy.

If you come home exhausted after sitting at a desk all day, it is likely that you were not so much bogged down in work as in thought.

Complaints of fatigue are among leading reasons we consult doctors (seven million consultations each year). Many factors cause fatigue, but any break from thinking revitalizes. Your practice can be like plugging into a battery charger. Have you noticed an energy boost?

Self-test 16: Wake-up Calls?

Sounds disrupt practice, but a car's horn or barking dog can also alert you, call you back if you have drifted away. Can you use distractions as wake-up calls.

Self-test 17: Are You Feeling Less Time Pressure?

In a poll, people asked: "How long is the present moment?" said: "three seconds." Time pressure goes with this.

Time is the space we think in. If it is cluttered we feel we have less time. When mental noise quiets, mental space frees up. Awareness brings timeless now where the pressure is off.

Are you feeling less time pressure?

Self-test 18: Are You "One thought away from life?"

I heard someone say: "Our memories are all we have and all we are." Do you agree?

If you do, your awareness is very low. If memories are all you have and all you are you may be missing the present completely. You may be as Ram Dass put it: "always one thought away from life."

Awareness alone fills our emptiness. It is more gratifying than any thought could possibly be. As awareness grows, memories become a smaller part of what you have and what you are.

Self-test 19: Use Your "Magic Slate."

I had a Magic Slate as a child. No matter how many marks I made on it I could clear them away and start fresh. Your exercise works like this. You do not have to heal your past. Enter the present and lo and behold, your slate is clean.

Bring to mind some small thing that bothers you: an irritating remark or a pet peeve. After practice, bring it to mind again.

Are you less distressed thinking of it now? Are you surprised it ever upset you? That is your Magic Slate in action, a taste of liberation to come.

Self-test 20: What are you Missing?

Try this. Stop reading. Look straight ahead and close your eyes a minute.

How did your experience change?

Now suppose a baby looking straight ahead suddenly closed its eyes. Imagine how dramatic the change would be. If nothing changed for you, you were not in the here and now, not aware.

Without awareness what is outside can not get in and the best of what we are is barely alive because what is inside can not get out. What are you missing? Master Deac says: "The past is a cancelled check; the future is a promissory note, and the present is payday." You are missing payday. If nothing changes when you close your eyes you can not imagine what you are missing.

Self-test 21: "Inner Music?"

Are you uncomfortable when silence comes over a room? Do you keep talking even when there is nothing to say? Do you want constant radio or TV?

We sometimes use noise to mask emptiness.

Our mental space is choked with continuous chatter to which we don't even listen. It's simply there to fill the vacuum. When the noise stops there is no inner music to take its place (Lindburg, *Gift from the Sea,* 1955, page 42).

When awareness is restored and the empty container fills, inner music sounds and you will not want noise anymore.

Self-test 22: A Simpler Life?

A magazine article listed 92 ways to simplify your life. Number one was "meditate."

Practice well and you might not need 91 others. The voluntary simplicity movement seeks "a world of peace and ease." Peace and ease have more to do with what is going on in your head than what is going on in your life. Order mind, and your world comes to order. Are things simpler now?

Self-test 23: Visit a Gallery.

Visit an art gallery and eavesdrop. Hear what goes on in people's minds as they view paintings. It is a running commentary of names, labels, judgments and opinions, much like what normally goes on in our minds.

Now walk the gallery and view the art. Can you see what is before your eyes or are you running commentary?

Self-test 24: Touch a Tree.

Find a tree in a secluded woods or park. Touch the tree the way a baby explores things. Lean on it and feel its strength. Stroke your face with a leaf.

Do you find pleasure here?

You would if you were aware. Note down your experience for later.

Self-test 25: What is *Your* Answer?

"Do you hear the grasshopper which is at your feet," asks the Kung Fu Master?

"How is it that you hear these things old man?" the boy responds.

"Young man, how is it that you do not?" the Master answers.

Can you answer the Master's question: "How is it that you do not?"

To find the answer, stop and listen. Hear the noisy tenant thinking morning till night, in the shower, through breakfast, driving to work, in line at the store. This blocks awareness like a solid wall. We have a signal-to-noise ratio problem, "signal" being sight and sound and simple truth before our eyes.

How did the Master hear the grasshopper?

As Master Deac says: "It is all awareness! Awareness! Awareness!"

Self-test 26: Noticing Low Awareness?

Do you ever notice low awareness?

In the course of a day we range from low to no awareness, but we do not sense this. When you do, do not be discouraged. Realizing low awareness *is* awareness, a good sign.

Self-test 27: Are you freeing your body?

Have you noticed a lighter step or improved posture?

Thinking weighs you down. Awareness lifts the world off your shoulders. As burdens lighten, body is liberated too. Are you freeing your body?

Self-test 28: Time to smell the flowers?

They say "we need time to smell the flowers." Is it *time* we lack?

Recall the last time you were in a room with flowers. Had you not seen them, would you have known they were there by the fragrance?

Having time to smell the flowers is good, but first and foremost we need the capacity. We need awareness.

Self-test 29: What Have You Seen?

A young man traveled far hoping to study with a renowned Zen Master. Meeting him, the Master asked: "Have you seen the auspicious vision (enlightenment)?"

"No," came the answer, "but I have seen a lawn chair."

From this the Master knew the young man's promise.

Why should seeing a lawn chair impress a Master?

It meant the young man, at least once had seen what was before his eyes.

What have you seen that you formerly missed even though it was right there? In time you may see another world.

Self-test 30: How much pleasure are you missing?

Zen Master Toni Packer asked a man what led him to meditate. He said the highlight of his week had always been Sunday breakfast: a perfect cup of coffee; egg and toast done just so. Then one Sunday "his breakfast was gone!"

You may not hear the noise in your head but you can know it is there by lack of pleasure in your life. 3D, surround sound and living color are pleasures missed daily. "The world is so full of a number of things," wrote the poet, "I'm sure we should all be as happy as Kings!" The poet was right. The state of awareness, as Brother Lawrence put it, is "all-sufficing," all we need for happiness. Missing those things, "reality-TV" is more interesting than living. We need to bungee-jump to feel alive.

We are "standing on a whale, fishing for minnows" as a Malaysian saying puts it. Review your day. How much pleasure did you miss? Did you see beauty in trees? If you walked blindfolded and someone told you you passed a row of maples, in terms of beauty would your experience be about the same as if you saw them? Did you feel the soft warmth of lips kissed goodbye; enjoy a sunrise on the way to work; feel comfort when you sat down in the chair to read?

The lower your awareness, the greater your distance is from pleasure. We miss beauty, not because it is subtle or faint, but because we are impermeable. A glance and dismiss relationship with a sunrise means you are missing payday.

Self-test 31: Can you be "Free as a Bird?"

One day I met a woman at my office door. As she approached a bird flew overhead. "I want to be like that," she said.

Inside she told me her worries. Her husband was taking on too much work and she feared for his health. Her teenage son had questionable friends. Winter was approaching and she dreaded driving in the snow.

As she talked I thought of the bird she envied. There were similarities in their lives. The bird was in danger from the neighbor's cat. Its food supply was uncertain and winter posed a threat. Their lives had similarities but one vital difference made her envy the bird. The bird was not living in its head. It was not cut off from the natural world, missing the vibrant now. The bird *was* free. Its freedom however, was not in its wings but in its silence.

Can you be free as a bird?

You can. This freedom is your birthright as the next chapter shows. Awareness is all you need.

CHAPTER THREE
"ORIGINAL PERFECTION:" A BABY'S AWARENESS

Raise your eyes and look about...
You shall be radiant at what you see.

Isaiah 60: 1-6

Whateveryou need to know: You were born aware, born knowing how to be happy. You still have what it takes. The way to your mansion is a return trip home.

I had an enlightened teacher. From the first I knew I was in the presence of my superior. She was so alive, so loving, so intuitive, spontaneous and full of joy. She was my baby. In this chapter I share her teachings.

I had not expected enlightenment in a baby. In fact I had expected very little. I thought I would see the absence of things. Instead I discovered a rare presence. What clued me in to this was her happiness.

When she was old enough to hold herself up by the crib rail, a rapid pulsed squeak-squeak-squeak-squeak came from her room each morning. Peeking in I saw her jumping up and down. She wore a blissful whole-body smile that upturned her chin and swept me up in her happiness. Her room was bright even on dark days. Could she have been glowing? Why was she so happy? The mystery haunted me until one winter night I found the answer.

That night a storm caused a power failure. The house temperature dropped. I must have overheated her bath to compensate and when her little feet touched the water she shrieked so loud it left me trembling. I skipped the bath and dressed her, all the while expecting an awful night with an upset infant. When she was dressed however, and our eyes met, I saw something amazing. She wore a great big ready-for-fun grin, just as if nothing had happened. Suddenly I understood her happiness. My tiny baby had Great Liberation.

Tiny Baby—Great Liberation

The hot bath water had been a painful shock for my baby, but when the trauma was over she was free. She was not stewing: "Of all the #%!$#@#! She burnt my feet! If this ever happens to me again I'll…!" She was not re-living the experience, keeping it current the way adults do. Leaving the past in its place she set herself free.

After first seeing this freedom I noticed it often. I saw it when she had the hiccups, for instance. Between hiccups she was serene and calm, not cursing each one, dreading the next and wondering how long they would last. She was not trapped in the concept of having hiccups, not confined to the mind-made reality adults live in. She had hiccups often but was free of them just the same.

Great Liberation is freedom from the tenant's noise. Freedom from thinking explained her happiness. It meant nothing blocked awareness. She had full access to the sources of true happiness. This made her a "filled container" with eyes open to beauty, senses to pleasure, a heart to love and a mind to truth. Let me show you how large we can be. Let me to tell you about my baby.

- Eyes Open to Beauty

We were caught in a downpour my toddler and I, rushing down a driveway of crushed stone. Suddenly her hand slipped from mine. She dropped to the ground and picked up a tiny stone. It was blue and speckled pink like a robin's egg. Not minding the rain she squatted there marveling at it. Her eyes were open to beauty even in a mad dash.

My favorite photo of my daughter shows an infant gazing in ecstasy at a shiny mobile above her crib. Evidently she saw more than adults see. She saw the overhead light in her bath water; the rainbow in a fly's wing. I think she saw through poet's eyes:

> *Ultra-pink peony…*
> *Silver Siamese soft-cat…*
> *Gold-dust butterfly…*(Buson)

She had no judgment or opinion about beauty. No favorite color made others lesser in her sight. Beauty outside flowed in and beauty inside flowed freely out. She was endlessly creative because creativity *is* awareness: awareness of endless possibilities. Gowns and "agushas" were some of her creations.

Gowns and "Agushas"

At age two, when she dressed her little doll she never used the clothes it came with. She used instead one of her father's white handkerchiefs. With this she draped sheathes, gowns and tunics with fluid ease, and with the same fluid ease moved on to the next design. She never showed me her creations. She took no pride in them. Nobody was there who needed credit. She never saved her creations because she did not need to. Nobody was there who feared loss. She set her designs free because she was free.

At age three, one summer day she came in from outside with a gift for Mommy. It was a white paper cup filled with fine soil, carefully smoothed and set with a dry twig and a few pebbles just so. Summer was in full bloom then and my first impulse was to ask: "Why no flowers?" I caught myself and was glad of it. This was no flower pot.

"What is this?" I asked, and right away I regretted asking. It was obvious what it was. It needed no name. But she was very bright and eagerly complied: "It's an agusha (a-gu-sha)," she said.

She made many agushas that summer with the same delicate care, and she always avoided color. As with the handkerchief she preferred simplicity. I think she chose simplicity the way photographers do where black and white reveals deeper elements of form and balance. Her tiny landscapes were miniature Zen gardens.

- Senses Open to Pleasure

I had to be vigilant on summer mornings. She liked nothing more than to run outside, arms outstretched, wearing only a smile, going as fast and as far as she could before I caught up to her. Imagine feeling that free!

With each day's waking, a new life of pleasure began for her. When I set her down she ran off gleefully. If I picked her up and set her facing the other way she ran off just as happily in the opposite direction. She was not happy because she was headed for this or that. She had bliss and peace unchanging. Her play was spontaneous and the world was a playground. She had still moments too and I never interrupted these. To me they seemed sacred.

We try to "get pleasure out of things," but it does not work that way. Happiness flows out, not in, out-flowing from a filled container. My baby had as much fun riding in the car to the party ("Weeeeeeeee!") as at the party. She had as much fun waiting in line to go on a ride as on the ride. There was as much there to enjoy because *she was all there to enjoy it*.

When she was two or so I did a television interview and was anxious to see myself on the evening news. She gave me ten seconds of viewing and then boisterously claimed my attention. When I tried to get her to watch me on screen her look said: "Are you crazy! I've got you *right here in person*!" How true it was, and how much more alive she was than I at that moment. After all, I had her there in person too.

I saw a baby at Fourth of July fireworks. Her mother could not get her to look up. The baby was enchanted by a key ring. She had awareness enough not to need fireworks. My little one never needed to be entertained. Everywhere she went the show played live in 3D; surround sound, and living color. Thoreau experienced this on retreat at Walden Pond when awareness made his life his "amusement, and never ceased to be novel." As he walked in the woods to see the birds and squirrels, he walked "in the village to see the men and boys. Instead of the wind among the pines I heard the carts rattle."

On rainy days my little girl rode her tricycle in circles in the garage, grinning ear to ear. She rode whole-heartedly. Later in life, reflexes ride. We are busy elsewhere. How could our play be other than half-hearted when more than half of us is missing?

<u>"Eyes to see and ears to hear"</u>

In Dickens' *Christmas Carol*, the enlightened Scrooge found "eyes to see and ears to hear:"

> *He walked about the streets, and watched the people hurrying to and fro, and looked down into the kitchens of houses, and up to the windows, and found that everything could yield him pleasure. He had never dreamed that any walk—that anything—could give him so much happiness.*

Scrooge saw nothing on this walk that had not been there before. Awareness made all things new.

My baby had "eyes to see and ears to hear." When she was small enough to fit in the basket with the clothes, we had a wonderful time on laundry day. I sang as I carried her up and down the stairs nestled in the bundles. My wide-eyed listener never looked at me and never reacted to or judged the song. To judge would have been to stand apart, to lose oneness with it. With no opinion to divide awareness, she was free to be the song itself. Her freedom let me sing without self-consciousness. I too could be the song itself. There could be no better audience.

In Zen they say: "If useless things do not hang in your mind, every season is a good season for you." Before concepts took control, my baby's mind was free. Unbiased by opinion, every season was good for her. Her pleasure was no less on dark than on bright days. Snow flakes were as welcome as summer showers. One day I saw her looking out the window watching the rain in awe: "Everything is getting all wet!" she said. She had seen rain many times before but she was seeing it now, again for the first time.

One rainy day she saw me reading the forecast on the Weather Channel. "What does it say, she asked?" I read it:

A huge area of rain covering almost all of New York State will continue to make this a miserable day.

-   Heart Open to Love

The other day I saw a man trying to get a smile from a baby. He was having no success, but he persisted as if nothing in his life was more important. Why do we want smiles from babies? It is because the smile is genuine. Real love flows like electrical current. It takes awareness to complete the circuit. Babies have the connection. A baby's love is real.

I forget her exact age, but for a time my baby loved everyone and greeted every man we passed on the street with an exuberant "Hi, Daddy!" Strangers passing by received generous gifts of love.

On Halloween I dressed her as a pumpkin and we walked hand in hand, door to door. Between houses I reached in her bag and took out the treats, every last one. When we finished she went home jubilant with an empty bag. Her happiness did not depend on candy or anything else. Awareness is all-sufficing. When aware, no emptiness needs filling. That is why she had so much love to give.

A Present for Jason

It had been a long shopping day but my toddler made no complaint. I promised her a toy or treat as a reward. I told her to choose anything she would like and asked her what she wanted. For some time she wondered and then she exclaimed: A present for Jason! Jason was our neighbors' newborn. I asked what the present would be and again she thought long. "A bathing suit," she shouted! We had a backyard pool and she loved to swim. She wanted the baby to share that happiness.

Choices born of awareness are not the same as those from thoughts of self. For my little one, a gift was something to give (not get). This caused confusion on her first visit to Santa. Her basic needs had always been met. She had no siblings to compete with and never wanted for anything. She was unprepared for Santa's question. "What do you want for Christmas," brought no response. Santa was speechless too. The room fell silent and I was about to intervene when she said: "Anything you give me I will be happy with." What did she want? She wanted *Santa* to be happy. She already was! She had the real thing, the happiness that comes free.

Later someone asked her: "What do you want *to be* when you grow up?" I sensed a better question might have been: "What do you want *to give?*" Happiness equals the degree of outflow from an open heart. Her natural giving was happiness itself.

A Child's Empathy

When you are aware you can feel another person's feelings. I saw such empathy in my daughter. I remember standing in a circle of women at a social gathering. I held the baby and watched her look from one woman to the next as they chatted and smiled. Suddenly she stopped and fixed her gaze on one. This woman smiled pleasantly and talked like the rest, yet my baby wore a worried look. I knew what she saw and it was not visible on the surface. Two weeks earlier this woman had lost her husband.

I saw empathy in my little one's actions too. When we rented a movie, she refused to watch it until her father and I were there to see it too. She was not separate from us. Our happiness was her happiness.

Dr. Bernie Siegel tells of a child's empathy. His patient was a little girl with cancer. Her tests came back indicating that her treatment had not been effective. He was heartsick as he told her parents the awful news. The child said: "Don't feel bad. You did your best."

Awareness acts like a ground wire conducting love to where it is needed, to where there is pain. Nothing is more natural than desire to relieve suffering. Outflow of love is strongest when the suffering is greatest. I saw an impulse to relieve suffering in my daughter, even an impulse to heal.

One day when she was about two, I was working on a project in her room when I stopped and sat down. "What's the matter," she asked? "My foot hurts," I said. She crossed the room quickly, arms out stretched toward my foot. She had the confident air of someone who had fixed such problems countless times before.

A *healer*? My two-year old!

"What are you going to do?" I asked impetuously. The instant my question registered the healer vanished. She had no "idea" what she was doing. She had no concept of it. Her action arose from pure awareness. My question blocked the spontaneous flow. I went without the treatment and I never saw the healer again. I never went without her love though and I never had to earn it. It was there when the bath was too hot, the bottle too cold. Her love was unconditional. Many times I felt its power and more than once her presence was my sanctuary.

A Master's Inspiration

Through these precious years I knew I was in the company of a fully enlightened being. I recognized original perfection, as Buddhists call it, the original perfection of her human nature. No Master out-performed her. The fact that she did not speak seemed more proof of wisdom. I wanted to be as silent and free as she was.

I had little time to myself however, and finding practice time was a challenge. When she had just begun to crawl I tried something desperate. I childproofed a room and lay down and focused on a spot on the ceiling. She crawled around me a while. Then to my amazement she settled in and joined me. She sat with her back touching my head, her eyes wide open, stone still, doing exactly what I was doing. Unlike me however she needed no transition time to enter this peaceful state. We shared this experience every day until as a toddler she was too active to sit.

Like a true master she inspired me to practice. I found an opportunity at preschool gymnastic classes. I sat on the sidelines, cross-legged against the gym wall focusing on the glossy floor. Several toddlers waited there too. I sat apart from them hoping not to be disturbed. Wherever I sat however, they gravitated to me. My silence and stillness did not make them uncomfortable as it does adults. On the contrary they were drawn to it. With no formalities, not even eye contact, they crowded in, leaned on me and nestled in my lap. When time came to go they scrambled from my lap and ran off without a backward glance. They took strange liberty with me when I was in that state. I think they felt at home because I was home. Centered in a mansion of awareness I could be sanctuary for them.

- ## Mind Open To Truth

Master Deac teaches: life should be like "looking in a pool of water… We should see clear to the bottom." Awareness sees clear to the bottom. The teaching also says: the water should be *clear and cool*." This is the peace and ease that comes with awareness. An experience with my baby illustrates.

Before she could speak I explained things to her and saw understanding in her eyes. I recall an instance when she saw clear to the bottom. She was four or five months old and had a high fever and a rash. The doctor asked to see her in the emergency room. While driving there I explained where we were going and why. At the hospital I explained each action the doctor performed and the use of each instrument. A nurse mocked: "Who are you talking to?" I did not mind. The baby attended to my every word, absorbing it all into her silence. She was not word-bound. She went beneath words to where they came from. Her awareness penetrated their deepest meaning: things are as they must be and should be. All is well. She made no protest and afterward the doctor said he had never before seen a baby stay calm through this examination.

Thoreau wished he could be as wise as a baby. I know what he meant. Thinking is second nature but awareness comes first. Wisdom comes from the mouths of babes because nothing blocks their contact with reality. They see the truth before their eyes. More than once I tested her understanding with *koans*, Zen riddles that measure enlightenment. She saw through them with no confusion, no uncertainty and never gave them a second thought.

At age four we talked of God, on the nature of death and other deep subjects. She was still young enough to understand.

It is said that with enlightenment you "leave the world of confusion and illusion" for "the real world (David Chadwick, *Thank You And OK*, 1994)." Confusions and illusions are thoughts. The real world, the domain of awareness, was my baby's dwelling place.

"At-one-ment"

She was up to something and her father warned: "If you mess things up, don't come crying to me." She answered: "Well then who should I go crying to?" She knew she needed the union that is love.

Someone called this union "at-one-ment." It is the difference between *seeing* what is there and *being* what is there (as my baby was one with the song). Such union occurs when no thoughts break the connection. You need to be nonjudgmental like a baby. You need to let things be, but the noisy tenant can not. It names, labels and judges everything. It meddles and cannot behold. Awareness beholds. It embraces without touching. In the fullness of awareness, you experience *what is*.

Our spirit is like a clear mirror, thus it reflects the universe harmoniously.

Full awareness sees clear to the bottom. You are free to enter the world of peace and ease. Think how liberating it feels to say: "Oh, I see. I understand." This freedom, this awareness, was my baby's resting state.

Minds free, thoughts gone Brows clear, faces serene (Chuang Tzu, in Merton, 1965, page 61.)

One day looking deep in her eyes I saw the source of her freedom: nothing had to be said...now, or ever. No question needed answering. No confusion had to be resolved. No error needed correction. "Great Liberation" means being this aware, free as you were born. Today when I see a baby, something deep in me comes to rest. I know there is sanity.

Access Denied

Rachael Remen (1996) recalls childhood summers by the sea. Some of her most beautiful moments were watching white birds fly overhead, their wings transparent as they passed between her and the sun. Years later she walked the same beach and was disappointed. There were gulls everywhere eating garbage and making raucous noise. Only later did she realize that these were the white birds of her childhood. It was not the beach that had changed.

We start life in a mansion of life's riches. Soon we trade "silence as deep as eternity for speech as shallow as time." When concepts replace awareness we go from full to empty.

Someone counted and found that four-year-olds smile four hundred times a day; adults fifteen times. Smiles diminish as thought claims a monopoly on consciousness. We become preoccupied with thought for its own sake. Actions arise, not from awareness but from thoughts. Thoughts in turn arise from other thoughts. Cut off from reality we do not function right. We drift far from happiness.

I saw signs of the loss when my daughter was four or five. She would turn upside-down looking backward through her legs. She seemed to be searching for a fresh look, the look she was losing. Sometimes she spun like a dervish, trying to get high it seemed, the way she used to be.

Soon rain lost its enchantment. No longer was she dazzled by the beauty of a fly's wing. Bright pure awareness dimmed and clouded. Awe and wonder were replaced by "the usual meaningless mumble," as Dr. Remen called it. She grew estranged from the world she loved.

It is just as the man who
In the midst of water cries from thirst.
It is no different from the child of a rich household
Who goes astray in some poor village.

I saw poverty come to my little one. Losing awareness meant losing happiness. I wanted so to stop the loss. I wondered. If I could make her understand "at-one-ment," would this help? Alan Watts had a good way of expressing it. I decided to try, using his words.

I waited for the perfect day. I wanted a day with beauty enough to break through thinking on its own; beauty enough to mirror her soul.

The day came, an afternoon in golden autumn. The air itself was luminous and glistened as we walked in the woods. Yellow maple leaves swirled silently round us blanketing the ground. We walked in silence for some time, then sat down face to face on the earth's gold cushion. "I have something important to tell you," I said. I gestured to her: "This is your inside." Then outstretching my arms to the surroundings I said:

"and this is your outside." Her eyes widened and sparked with recognition of something momentous. For one joyous moment I thought I had gotten through. Then she said: "Do you mean to say *I own* all this property!"

Words were of no use. They built the wall that blocks awareness. The wall has to be taken down.

- Returning

A proverb says: "When the baby cries, it is either hungry or in pain." With basic needs met, a baby's happiness abounds. My little one had a secure two-parent-home and a loving Grandmother nearby, but there was nothing unusual about her life. This is not the story of one baby. This is *your* story too. We are so lost however, so far from our original nature that it is almost impossible to imagine where we started.

Consider the man who drove past you on the highway, cursing and shaking a fist. This man was once a baby: a beautiful bundle of joy. When he was out of sorts his mother knew he was suffering. "Something's wrong," she would say. "That's not my baby." Not happy, he was "not himself."

As he grew, joy faded and disappeared. He became like other adults, *not themselves at all*, throwing tantrums in living rooms and boardrooms, on telephones and on highways. It is impossible to see any joy at all in most adults, but that does not mean it is not there. Stars in the night sky seem to weaken and fade at dawn, but they have not weakened or faded, only receded from view. The same is true of the brilliance of your nature. You can be as you were born. You can raise your eyes and look about and be radiant at what you see. Awareness is all you need.

CHAPTER FOUR
CONFUSION AND ILLUSION: HOW CONCEPTS BLIND US

Be consistent with reality.

Master Choe

W<u>hat you need to know</u>: Early in life concepts take the place of awareness. Instead of acting out of awareness we "run" concepts blindly the way a computer runs programs. This blindness causes of most of life's pain. Awareness is the remedy.

I was introduced to karate briefly many years ago and I recall a strange sight. It was my teacher with a bandaged head and his arm in a sling. I asked how it happened and he blushed. On spring break in Florida he had walked past a bar just as a brawl spilled out. Suddenly engulfed in a street fight he completely forgot he knew karate. Instead of using his skill he did what the other brawlers were doing and he took a beating.

Our lives are something like this. We are born aware. Like my baby we know how to be happy. We have what it takes. Then we get confused like my karate teacher. We do what everyone else is doing and we take a beating. The trouble starts early when awareness is lost.

- <u>How Awareness is Lost</u>

One day at the aquarium I stopped to see a strange creature. It looked like a giant potato luxuriating in a small tank, and the manatee easily held my attention. As I stood watching, a stream of small children came by tugging their parents' sleeves. "What's that Daddy?" That's a manatee. "What's that Mommy?" "A manatee." They did not stop, but with a glance and a name rushed on to the next tank.

These little ones had a mission. They were pairing names with mental pictures, images of what they saw. In the "What's that Mommy?"

stage, children learn sixty new words per week. Images are stored in memory, each with its label: "manatee," "tree," "banana," "dog." These representations fill the mind which acts as a sort of display case. When someone says "manatee," the stored image appears. In this way we build mental representations of the world. We come to know the world, not through awareness but through concepts. In the process, without our knowing it, concepts become our reality. They become our (mind-made) world. When we lose awareness, we lose contact with reality.

-     Losing Awareness; Losing Contact with Reality

One day when my little one was about four, I had to work in the garden and she wanted to play in the house. She followed grudgingly. I gave her a small hoe and taught her how to use it. She worked the soil quietly a while, then suddenly shouted for joy: "Mommy! Mommy! Work is *Play*!" Her awareness won out over the "work" concept. If this had happened later in life however, it might not have.

When concepts take over, we lose awareness. We no longer see what is before our eyes; no longer have contact with reality.

"What is reality," a Zen student asks?

"The tree in the courtyard," the Master replies.

The student goes out and looks, but he does not see what is before his eyes. Instead recognition (re-cognition, thinking again) occurs. His tree concept re-presents itself. "A tree...he muses, nothing new." He wonders why the teacher can not give a straight answer. Naturally he is confused. He does not know his own blindness, does not know that he lacks awareness.

A study illustrates the source of his problem. Researchers altered playing cards. They made spades and clubs red, diamonds and hearts black. Observers were asked to identify the cards and were given brief exposures with a viewing machine. As images flashed before their eyes, observers reported standard cards: "two of diamonds, ace of spades," etc. Longer exposures did not change their reports. Over time some viewers became uncomfortable, even sick, but still reported standard cards. What they were seeing was their conceptions of cards. These concepts blocked awareness.

Rachael Remen said: "a label is a mask life wears." In this study, concepts like "ace of spades, two of diamonds," etc., masked what was there. In real life, "work" masks the play of gardening. A "tree" concept kept the Zen student from seeing reality when he looked at the tree in the courtyard.

Reliance on concepts (in the absence of awareness) makes confusion and illusion normal for us. This chapter shows how concepts blind us, and how the blindness we don't even know we have causes suffering.

How Concepts Blind Us

Master Deac often repeats a fundamental teaching: "Be consistent with reality." Our lives are not as consistent with reality as we assume. They are consistent with concepts instead. We act out of concepts, not out of awareness. We "run concepts" blindly the way computers run programs. Let me show you what I mean.

- Running Concepts: Miss Benning's Lesson

My daughter's first computer instruction came from a favorite teacher, Miss Benning. Miss Benning had students write instructions for doing simple things like making a peanut butter and jelly sandwich. Then she acted out their instructions, following them to the letter. If a student said: "spread the peanut butter on the bread," she did so without holding the bread in her hand. The slice slid and was torn. If a student said: "put the knife in the peanut butter" but did not say: "open the jar," she hit the lid with the knife again and again to no effect. If a student said "remove the lid" but not "place it on the table," she held both lid and jar in her hand making work impossible. Running these programs resulted in no sandwich and a big mess.

When a computer runs programs all steps are followed to the letter *no matter what*. We "run concepts" in the same way, doing what our concepts of reality specify, blind to the truth only awareness can see. Too often, this makes a big mess of our lives.

The concept of running programs may help us understand the mystery of anorexia. Someone suffering from this tragic illness acts out of the concept: "I need to lose weight." Run like a program, this concept decides what she thinks, what she does, and what she sees in the mirror. Others can see that her concept is inconsistent with reality. For the anorexic however, it is reality and the program's specifications are followed to the letter. The program (in the absence of awareness) runs no matter how grave the consequences.

Anorexia illustrates how programs run blindly as Miss Benning's lesson taught. It illustrates how our minds work in the absence of awareness. This applies to all concepts. Consider a program all of us run: the "age program."

Running the "Age" Program

I once heard a sixty-year old man describe his life as "gradual deterioration." That was two decades ago. For twenty years he has run a "gradual deterioration" program, his concept of age.

To varying degrees all of us run age programs. This deep seated concept sets up expectations, dictates actions and wields debilitating power of suggestion. As in anorexia, it defines reality for us and even decides what we see. At eighteen, for instance we see "freckles." At eighty we see only "age spots."

Our reality is mind-made, and the mind keeps our world in order. The mind needs to confirm that its concepts are real. Thus minor aches and pains are used to verify the age concept. "Just as I thought, old age," becomes our response to pain, shoring up our mind-made reality. Discomfort that meant nothing at twenty, at sixty becomes proof, confirmation of reality. Such "old age" self-suggestion is debilitating both physically and emotionally. (Subversive influence is inherent even in the question "How old are you?" We never ask "how young?")

We use concepts (not awareness) to define ourselves. When we "own up" to a particular age, it owns us just as the concept "I need to lose weight" owns the anorexic. It decides our actions. When the program specifies "act your age," at eighty we sit sedentary, deteriorating according to schedule. An octogenarian might see through the illusion and refuse to "own up to eighty." He might go skydiving, intentionally violating old age specifications, telling himself and the world: "'old' is not my reality." Programs run unconsciously however, and they are subversive. Unless awareness frees us, negative consequences of the age concept are inescapable.

Our age concept has sub-programs too. These tell us how to dress, where to go and with whom. Some dentists suggest duller yellow teeth for elderly patients, but no matter how limiting and self-destructive, we obey these programs. We age "to the letter."

Not long ago a finding that people in their nineties can build muscle made front page news. The finding surprised us because it violates our age concept. To "age" is to deteriorate: to lose, not gain muscle. The program sets up expectations of irreversible loss in muscle, bone mass, balance, flexibility, etc.

Karate dō offers a very different, positive view of aging. As Master Deac teaches, the body is preserved and perfected through disciplined Karate practice. ("Your body is your temple," cautioned Master Choe, "If you destroy it, where are you going to go?") Preserve yourself in this way and you "give life back to life." Sustained well-being and extended age span follow.

The tradition sees a one hundred year life span in five phases. In the first (birth to twenty years of age), we make mistakes and learn from them. In phase two (ages twenty to forty) we have "overcome the foolishness of youth." Our mistakes are not repeated. In the decades from forty to sixty we prosper, if not by wealth by experience, and wealth is not as important as what we have learned. An experienced leader emerges in the decades from sixty to eighty. Life's learning has positioned us where people will follow. Then comes "your gift," your reward for a wisely lived life, a fifth phase extending from eighty to one hundred years.

Master Deac proves by living example that this positive concept of age *is* consistent with reality. It accords with the ancient view of aging where *disuse*, not "age," is the cause of deterioration. In this view: "that which is used thrives and that which is not used wastes away." This concept (because it is consistent with reality) serves us far better than the "gradual deterioration" model. If we attribute muscle loss to disuse, not "age," the news about building muscle at ninety is not news at all. Awareness frees spontaneous action like building muscle for instance, instead of "acting our age," deteriorating according to plan.

Master Choe advised: "When you are ninety years old Deacsan, do not let anyone treat you like you are ninety years old." He meant stay free of the concept and its debilitating influence. Master Deac absorbed the lesson.

Enough awareness will override the toxic concept, shut the program down, and free us of the "age" specter. Like computers however, we lack awareness. We are blind to truth. Where a doctor's trained eye sees actual physical causes of ill-being, we see only "ravages of age." Doctors tell us that "no one dies of old age," yet we look and we are blind to this. As in anorexia, concepts dictate what we see.

Master Choe taught that concepts should be "fluid" not "solid." Fluid concepts would not harden into barriers that block awareness. The more solid our concepts, the more rigidly programs confine us. "Solid" concepts, run as programs are followed to the letter no matter how limiting and self-destructive. The more inconsistent with reality a concept is the more harm running its program is likely to do. Chapter Five shows how a self-interest program reduces our capacity for love. Chapter Thirteen suggests that a "religion program" may limit our experience of God.

Among such self-limiting programs are those discussed in the balance of this chapter. They stem from concepts of "mind" and "body." Let me show you how these concepts came into existence and the surprising amount of harm they do.

Mind-Body Programs and how they Harm Us

What do we think we are?

Different concepts of human nature have been held at different times in history. In the Golden Age of Greece, a human being was defined as "a living soul." The soul had "faculties" like digestion, movement, sensation and "mind" or thinking.

What we think we are today is something quite different. We believe ourselves to be a "mind" and a "body." "Body" is material or physical; the "mind" is not. We do not question these concepts of what we are. We see them as ultimate truth, ultimate reality. You may be surprised by where they came from.

The Origin of Mind-Body Concepts

The Golden Age was philosophy's richest era. Later thinkers saw themselves as mere dwarves on the shoulders of giants. They could see what the ancients saw, plus a little more. French philosopher Rene Descartes (1595 to 1650) however, wanted a philosophy of his own. He decided to approach the subject of human nature as if no one before him had ever considered it. The mind and body concepts he came up with cause trouble for us every day of our lives.

Descartes relied on rational thought in seeking the truth of human nature. He simply sat and thought, and any idea he could doubt was true, he rejected. Sitting in darkness he discarded everything he could possibly doubt. He dismissed all he had seen and heard. His senses may have failed him. He dismissed all he had been taught since it too might be in error. He even doubted that he was Rene Descartes. (Some "malicious demon" might be deceiving him.) After dismissing all he could doubt, only one thing remained that he could be certain of. He was certain he was thinking. Even when he doubted he was thinking he was thinking. This led to his famous conclusion: "I think, therefore I am."

With this Descartes proved he existed, but that was all he could say with absolute certainty. Trouble began when he went a step further and asked: "What am I?"

Descartes' answer to "What am I?" could be only this: a "thinking thing." This alone could he know with logical certainty. "I am a thinking thing," he said, "I am a mind." Here we became tenants, minds dwelling in physical heads, noisy tenants, "thinking things" by definition.

Formerly we saw vital souls with faculties of mind or thinking. Descartes used the words "soul" and "mind" interchangeably. He made *the soul* a "thinking thing." This mind (or soul), he said "has no need of body" and would "still be all it is even if the body ceased to exist."

At this time the Catholic Church wielded powerful influence. Descartes' "mind," since it was not physical and did not die with the body, gave the Church an immortal soul. This had much to do with acceptance of Descartes' concepts.

Now with mind separate from body, Descartes was left with a body that was isolated too. This is the "mind-body problem," a conceptual trap for philosophers and a very real problem for us. Let me explain the "body" concept and how body's isolation from mind causes endless trouble.

The Body Concept

In Descartes' time hydraulic technology was the latest thing. Palace gardens were adorned with manikins powered by water in pipes. These animated mechanisms moved, gestured and even spoke. Descartes' "body" concept was inspired by these. He argued that if people could build machines like these, God could certainly build machines like bodies. He defined "body" accordingly as "pipes, pulleys, levers, beams, sieves, strainers and coverings," etc., all mechanical; all operating independent of mind.

If body is separate from mind however, how is it that when we decide to walk the body actually moves? Descartes' concepts did not allow interaction of mind and body. This problem was circumvented by the notion of "Divine Intervention." It was proposed that when the mind decides to walk, God moves the body.

Descartes' ideas were not welcomed by everyone. Some of his contemporaries saw his ideas as ridiculous. One wrote: "Descartes is a whim and a wham without one why or wherefore, a fellow that invented ridiculous principles of his own, and now expects us to believe them as truth."

A comical riddle was made of the philosophy:

What is body? Never mind.
What is mind? No matter.
What is soul? It is immaterial.

It took many years yet in time we did adopt Descartes' concepts. A mechanical body and a separate, independent mind became ultimate truth for us, ultimate reality. When they did, concepts highly inconsistent with reality became major programs run by everyone. Let me explain how Descartes' mind-body concepts harm us.

Mind-Body Problems

Just as an "age" concept determines what we think, see and do, mind-body concepts control thoughts and actions. One consequence is that these concepts make us see ourselves as victims of ills we actually cause. Consider the "victim program."

- Running the "Victim Program"

The ills I refer to here are the "dis-ease" mentioned earlier. Some call it "psychosomatic" (psycho-mind; soma-body) illness. We see more doctors for these everyday ills than for any other health problems. Estimates put seventy to ninety percent of illness in the "stress-related "category. Our biggest-selling prescription drugs treat anxiety and ulcers. Sixty-three percent of adults have trouble with insomnia, and we spend one hundred billion dollars annually on pain care for headaches and other pain.

Steve Allen made a joke of it:

Are you bothered by splitting headaches?
Do as countless others do. Suffer.

"Living with" these problems, as we tend to do, is a bit like walking around with a tack in your shoe.

"A tack in the shoe"

I once worked in a hospital and entering at shift change I noticed a coworker limping. The next day I saw the same limp and a few days later it was still there. I asked what was wrong. "A tack in the shoe," he said.

This mystified me. How odd that he would live with the pain. Pain serves a purpose. It is meant to call us to awareness. Pain says: "There's a problem. Fix it!" For self-preservation it sounds an alarm, calling you to awareness so you can stop the damage. In not answering the call, the man with the tack made himself helpless, made himself a victim.

All pain has purpose as guidance. Whether it is pain from a tack in the shoe or from headaches, ulcers or muscle tension, pain is a call to awareness. We "live with" pain when we assume the call is not for us, that is, when we disown the pain and deny responsibility. Our choice of words when describing such ills explains what I mean.

We deny responsibility when we say: "My stomach is bothering me." (We never say "I am bothering my stomach.") Underlying concepts tell us that the stomach operates independently. We say: "My nerves are giving me trouble." ("I am troubling my nerves" would make no sense to us.) The "mind-body program" specifies no mental influence.

Thus we refer "the call" to the doctor or pharmacist, hoping not to hear it again. These ills then become chronic, the unanswered call to awareness being repeated. In denying responsibility we miss something we need: we miss the guidance life's pain offers. That guidance is pain's meaning and purpose. (In Chapter Seven we will see how answering the call might remedy such problems and prevent their return.) Missing the call we walk around like the man with a tack in his shoe. Instead of healing ourselves we make ourselves victims. Concepts blind us to the cause of our ills though evidence of such causation is everywhere.

Evidence of Causation?

Descartes' concepts forbid mind-body interaction. Psycho-somatic research however, documents emotional influence in numerous diseases.

Fascinating research was conducted in the 1960's by David Graham and colleagues. They found that certain illnesses went with specific attitudes, thoughts and feelings. An ulcer attitude for instance was: "I'm not getting my fair share." In an ulcer you literally "eat yourself up inside" when stomach acids digest a portion of the stomach lining. Graham's findings suggest that ulcers are the work of the noisy tenant. Ulcers seem to come right off the assembly line of a stress manufacturing plant: the thinking mind.

Here are some other illnesses with their associated attitudes. Hives: felt he was taking a beating and was helpless to do anything about it. Acne: felt he was being picked on and wanted to be let alone. Asthma: felt left out in the cold and wanted to shut the person or situation out. Constipation: felt in a situation from which nothing good could come but kept up with it grimly. Essential hypertension: felt threatened with harm and had to be ready for anything. Low back pain: wanted to run away. Vomiting: felt something wrong had happened, usually something for which he felt responsible, and wished it had not happened and wanted to undo it.

The ancient Greeks said: "the colon is the mirror of the mind." Considering Graham's findings, this phrase seems to apply to organs throughout the body. The body is an echo chamber resonating feelings. Our presumed "mechanical breakdowns" are in fact uniquely human problems. They are there to guide us. "Watch what you are doing," the body cries. "See what brings pain." The deep-rooted concepts however, that tell us what is real, forbid body this role. Thus in the case of ulcers, when a microbe was found present in the ulcer process, explanations involving mental causes were instantly dropped. News reports pronounced that the "*real* cause of ulcers" (italics are mine) had finally been found. My book *Where Medicine Fails* (1986) traced the history of such blindness, showing that despite new evidence, opinion always reverts to the set-in-stone specifications of the mind-body program.

Our concepts are like piles set in concrete at the base of buildings. They hold it in place and we do not know they are there. Underlying concepts of human nature, concepts that dictate the programs we run have similar hold on us. They are never questioned. We don't even know they are there. Truth that would shake the foundations of beliefs, the reality before our eyes, cannot be seen. Through centuries of medical history, evidence of mind-body interaction has been either ignored or denied. Any "real" illness has a physical cause.

Thus blaming dumb mechanism we miss pain's message. The physical cause is the real cause, keeping us helpless. Mental influence is ruled out creating an illusion of victimization. It seems we are not so much "victims of stress" as we are victims of ignorance, and the problem does not end here. Consider the "mental" side of the mind-body coin. Here too we have made ourselves victims.

Victims of Our Thoughts?

As a mechanical body concept makes us see ourselves as victims of our bodies, Descartes' concept of mind makes us see ourselves as victims of our thoughts. Let me explain how.

Descartes said: I am a thinking thing. I am a mind. If I *am* a mind, mind is not mine to govern. When I have troublesome thoughts, I am not responsible for them. If my thoughts are not mine to control, I become their helpless victim.

Philosophers of the Golden Age saw this differently too. "I am a living soul," they said, and "I *have* mental faculties." If I *have* mind, emotion, thought and reason, I am not a victim of my thinking. I am responsible for my thoughts. This view empowers us as reflected in the Biblical teaching: "He that ruleth his spirit is better than he that taketh a city (Proverbs 16:32)."

A poet wrote: "Dame Nature doubtless has designed a Man the Monarch of his Mind." This view that we are responsible for our thoughts seems consistent with the intelligent design in nature. It is consistent with the notion of free will. Descartes' concepts however, took responsibility for our thoughts away from us. Once presumed Monarchs of Mind we came to see ourselves as helpless. This is how we came to see ourselves as victims of our thoughts. This is, of course, no simple matter to resolve, but perhaps our concept of "mental illness" could benefit from a fresh look. Prospects for mental health become more hopeful in the light of awareness.

- No Self-healing

According to Descartes' concept of body, healing is a mechanical process. Thus "self-healing," like other forms of mental influence, is ruled out of play despite ample evidence of its existence.

Richard Moss (1997) tells of Rachael, a woman with advanced pancreatic cancer. The cancer was diagnosed shortly before her wedding. She was expected to live no longer than a month or two. After the wedding she told her loved ones she wanted time alone. She told them not to be alarmed by tears or by shouts that might come from her room. She wanted to become intimate with her experience of this illness.

Rachael retreated to her room and spent time in silence. She blindfolded her eyes and listened to the day to deepen experience. She freed herself of concepts of "cancer, irreversible, terminal." These became just words to her. Instead of worrying about her pain she sang and danced it. She had a recurrent dream of falling and stood on her dresser and fell on her mattress. Complying with an inner sense, right action arose spontaneously. Her pain eased and ended and her strength returned. Dr. Moss said: "All she had to do was listen."

Rachael did not run the "victim" program. She allowed awareness to guide her. The chauffeur took the wheel. She said she lived "like an animal" (free as a bird). To the astonishment of her doctors the cancer disappeared. After ten years Dr. Moss reported that she remained well.

Why does a report like this astonish us? Why is it so mysterious?

It is so because it violates our concept of reality. It is out of sync with mechanical bodies uninfluenced by mind and emotion. Our concepts make no provision for self-healing and so it seems unreal. Without a conceptual hold on something, in our mind-made reality, it simply cannot exist.

Pioneers in the field of psychosomatic medicine saw evidence of mind-body interaction. They thought their research findings would revolutionize medicine. Instead, events in conflict with the mind-body program (like Rachael's self-healing), have been seen as medical curiosities. "Spontaneous remission" is the term applied to unexplained instances of healing where "spontaneous" implies that the body acts alone. Surely the "helpless victim" could not be responsible. We can see what our programs specify and no more.

Yogic feats like altering body temperature and suspending breathing are well documented. So is healing with meditation (*Meditation as Medicine,* Khalsa, 2002). The most powerful demonstration of our power to control body is seen in meditation Masters who announce the day and time of their departure from life. Surrounded by friends and followers, they pass on voluntarily. We have unthinkable power over body, *unthinkable* because our concepts forbid it.

Descartes' mental inventions have made us victims, blind to the fact that we cause our own dis-ease. Self-healing power lies dormant in us and without awareness will remain so. Last but not least, another harmful consequence of Descartes' concepts must be noted. Life's pain is meaningless suffering. Pain is guidance unseen.

-    <u>Meaningless Suffering: Missing the Call</u>

Pain's meaning and purpose is guidance. Pain speaks in the body's voice: "There's a problem. Fix it." Headache and ulcer pain, like pain from a tack in the shoe, calls us to awareness. Answer the call and awareness guides us. As Chapter 7 shows, it brings understanding and acceptance that can move us in the direction of love. When this occurs, pain's purpose is served.

Seeing only faulty mechanism we miss pain's guidance. We see mechanical failure with no more meaning and purpose than a flat tire. Our suffering is meaningless and pain is life's garbage. We just want to be rid of it.

Answer pain's call to awareness however, and there need be no meaningless suffering in your life. Healing becomes possible just as awareness makes it possible to fix the problem of a tack in your shoe. You see the true source of pain and how to remove it. With awareness you might avoid the same pain in the future. Both healing and prevention become possible.

With awareness you stop running the "mechanical body" program. You see things differently. It is as if you are an orchestra conductor. The instruments are your stomach, heart, lungs, muscles, glands, vessels, etc. Each instrument plays its part (stomach secretes acid, heart pumps blood, etc.). You the conductor however, set the tone and tempo. You create harmony or dissonance; balance or imbalance, ease or dis-ease. If you listen to your body you will hear the performance you are conducting. You may discover that you are not a "victim" of stress, but have been in control all along without knowing it.

When awareness reveals pain's meaning and purpose, enlightened thoughts and actions follow, awareness providing the remedy. Master Deac teaches that pain can make you stronger. Our blindness stands in the way of finding that strength.

Concepts, the masks life wears, confuse and misdirect us. Descartes' mind and body concepts are a legacy of helplessness. We see helplessness in our belief that we are victims of problems we actually cause. We see helplessness in our denial of self-healing power. We see helplessness in our meaningless suffering, our blindness to pain's meaning and purpose.

In all this we are like the confused karate teacher, confused without knowing we are confused. We do not know what we are. Look to this ignorance for the source of most of life's pain.

The problem is vast and complex. The solution however, is simple. Restore awareness and concepts become fluid. Rigid programs release their hold and shut down. New possibilities emerge, hopeful prospects of self-healing and of a higher standard of sanity. The "freedom from ignorance" sought in meditation tradition is freedom from concepts that block the light of truth. To be liberated, awareness is all you need.

The Solution: Awareness

That day at the aquarium a younger child stayed, face to the glass, glowing with pleasure. His arms fluttered with the manatee's fins; his head tilted when the creature spun. He did not know its name. He did not care to. His intimate knowing gratified more. He was not just seeing the manatee. He was being the manatee. When his mother called he did not answer. He protested when his father pulled him away.

Awareness is another way of knowing. It is being at one with reality, free of confusion and illusion.

In the silence at Walden Pond Thoreau saw the confusion and illusion caused by thinking. He said we need a "realometer" a way to tell what is real. Awareness is it.

As the proverb says, "thinking is very far from knowing." In his search for truth Descartes never stopped thinking. Suppose he had. What would he have seen? Beneath thoughts and concepts he would have found awareness. Awareness would have shown him that something is wrong with the question: "What is human nature?" It would have seemed like a tree asking: "Am I a maple or a pine? Should I shed my leaves or should I not?" Had Descartes seen clear to the bottom he would have seen the limitations of thought, and the limitless power of awareness to know.

"Leave the world of confusion and illusion for the real world," said a Zen Master. "Be not confused," said Master Choe. "It surrounds you. It will become part of you." Awareness is all you need.

CHAPTER FIVE
SELF-INTEREST AND THE ILLUSION OF LOVE

Always be a giver and a non-taker.

The Laws of Manu

What you need to know: Our concept of "self" sets up a program, a self-interest agenda that sends us the wrong way in pursuit of happiness. Running the program limits our capacity for love. The solution is awareness.

When my daughter was four we had a visitor one day, a boy who was learning to read. She showed him her books and he picked one up and sounded out the title: "My...Little...Sto-ry...Book." "No," said my daughter, alarmed. "That's *my* little storybook." The boy pointed to the title and read again, this time with authority: "My Little Story Book. Nooooo...," shrieked my daughter. "That's my little storybook. *My* little storybook! Mine! Mine! Mine! Mine! Miiiine!"

The natural giver had turned around and the new direction took her further from happiness than she had ever been.

What happened? What accounted for the turn around?

The wisdom of Karate dō answers this question.

"Seeing yourself:" The Problem of Self-interest

In the sixteenth century the need for fighting skills in the Orient diminished and martial arts developed an emphasis on spiritual growth. The ending *do* meaning "the way" was given (*ken-do, judo, aikido*), and the *dojo* became "The Place of Enlightenment" (Hyams, pages 2-4). Karate dō took form in this context. Its sword of wisdom cuts through our problem of "self" and self-interest.

Master Deac teaches: "Life should be like looking in a pool of water, clear and cool. We should see clear to the bottom." He adds: "we should not see ourselves in it."

When you see yourself in a pool of water you see only a reflection. It has no substance. It is not real, but if you see yourself *it is all you can see.* Your view of reality, your access to the truth before your eyes is cut off. Self-consciousness, self-absorption and self-interest take the place of awareness. See yourself, and you no longer see clear to the bottom. You see yourself alone.

It happens to all of us. We start life in a mansion of awareness. Out of the abundance, giving comes naturally and happiness comes free. Poverty enters when awareness is lost. Our natural capacity for happiness diminishes. That capacity is also our ability to love.

From then on, some degree of emptiness is always felt. A need to fill it emerges, but that need is impossible to satisfy because a self-interest program sends us the wrong way. Born givers become takers. Our pursuit of happiness goes contrary to our nature and therefore fails. The definition sums it up: unhappiness is wanting something for yourself.

The trouble starts with seeing ourselves in it; with thoughts of self. Webster's definition of "self" has two parts. First: "one's own person as distinct from all others." This concept of a lone self disconnects and isolates us. The second part of the definition is: "one's own welfare, interest or advantage." Here the lone self becomes a needy taker. "Giving" has no place in this concept of what we are. Instead a "taker program" follows. That program specifies self-gratification as the way to happiness.

This is how it comes to be that a self-interest agenda sends us contrary to our nature, opposite love. The problem is deeper and more far reaching than you might guess. The solution however, as before, is simple. This chapter explores self-interest and the illusion of love, and points to the answer: awareness.

Self-interest and the Illusion of Love

It was a bad hair day and I tried a new shop for a cut. I had barely met the hairdresser when I started complaining: "What I want is so simple. I can't see why it's so hard to get." Without knowing it I was making her anxious. When I saw this I was ashamed and wanted to undo the damage. I told her any cut would be fine. Then I closed my eyes and while she cut I directed love to her, holding her in my attention, silently wishing her well.

When she stopped cutting I opened my eyes and saw to my amazement the best haircut I had ever had. Then instantly my concern for the hairdresser vanished. I was interested in me now. I thought I had the secret of a great haircut. Love the hairdresser! I thought I was set for life.

I made another appointment and in a few weeks eagerly returned. I asked the woman for the same cut. Then I closed my eyes and set out to project love. This time it was harder to stay focused but I kept it up, and I thought I had done fairly well. When she stopped cutting I opened my eyes to a greater surprise than the first had been. It was the worst haircut ever, with mismatched sides and so short it was actually cut above the hairline.

There are no accidents. I knew instantly I was being guided. I was being taught some lesson here, but what could it be? I walked through the mall and into the parking lot dazed. Finally the fog cleared. I stood in awe at what I discovered. What I had called "love," what I had actually *felt as love,* was not love at all. It was love's opposite! It was self-interest and self-gratification. I had mistaken taking for giving.

The lesson hit like a sledgehammer and I needed just that. I had made the same mistake before. I remembered an experience from high school. My class had prepared Christmas baskets for the needy and I could not wait to deliver them. When the day came we loaded our cars and drove to the old part of the city. I knocked at the door at the first address and a man answered. To my surprise he refused the gift. I was turned away again at the next apartment. Some classmates were turned away too. Did we have the wrong addresses? I carried the list with me to one door and pointed to the name. The man shook his head: "It's a mistake," he said. At another a woman snapped: "Leave it on the step," and shut the door abruptly. I did not understand what happened that day. Now, thanks to a bad haircut I did.

The "joy of giving" I thought I felt was only an illusion of giving. I wanted to be a "good deed doer." I wanted have-nots so I could be a have. The high I felt was more self-gratification than love. It may have been the same illusion of love I had on the day of that haircut. Without knowing it, I was going the wrong way.

Imagine water flowing through a hose. The flow can go in only one direction. Self-interest goes contrary to love. One takes; one gives. Intake and outflow cannot exist at the same time. These two are opposites, yet the feeling of self-gratification can make them hard to distinguish. This is a major problem. Let's see how deep it goes.

- "Confusion and Illusion" about Love

How much of what we call "love" is self-gratification, self-interest in disguise?

Abe Lincoln had a favorite riddle: "How many legs would a dog have if you called a tail a leg? Five? No, four because calling a tail a leg doesn't make it a leg." Consider what we call "love" in song lyrics.

"I want you; I need you, I love you." "My heart aches with love for you." A lone and needy self cries out here. Self-interest aches, not love.

"When will love come my way" implies waiting to *get* love. Love however, is something to *give*. Wanting to get love, it cannot possibly outflow. Wanting love, it cannot exist.

How about: "If you don't treat her right she won't love you tonight." Self-interest dominates here, along with confusion that arises when "love" and "sex" are used as interchangeable words.

"Say you love me," says another song, "say those pretty words and I will give my love to you." Why do partners need to hear: "I love you?" It is because the words bring self-gratifying self-assurance. They are taken as evidence of love, and evidence is needed when proof is lacking.

"Looking in the eyes of love" is a popular lyric. How many people love the image of themselves reflected in adoring eyes? Here the good feeling of self-gratification is easily confused with love. Someone who is "full of himself" has no room for another.

"Darling please adore me" shows the same self-interest agenda with its need to take, get, have and keep love. In truth we need *to love*. Gratification is outflow, not intake. Love cannot be taken. It can only be received in gracious acts of awareness, and it is given in the same way. We could hardly be more confused.

Everyday use of the word shows more evidence of going the wrong way. "I love you because you make me proud. I love you because you care for me." These phrases make love conditional on getting something for oneself. Again here, feelings of self-gratification create an illusion. Calling it "love" does not make it love.

Marriages of "give and take" show the same confusion. Water cannot run in two directions at once. Only give and give could possibly be love.

The sage said: "Always be a giver and a non-taker." He said *always* with good reason. Where there is taking there is no love, no real love, no true happiness. But despite repeated failure, despite heartache and heartbreak when we see ourselves in it, the self-interest program like a broken compass continues to send us the wrong way.

Erich Fromm said: "To analyze the nature of love is to discover its general absence (*The Art of Loving*, 1956)." What are we missing? Compare the light and warmth of the sun with that of a star. We are suns by nature. We shine dimly however, like stars. These Self-tests might suggest to you the possibility of something more in you, something you are missing, something that awaits awareness.

Love Tests

* In intimate moments does your lover need to hear the words "I love you?" (Yes. No.)

Looking in your eyes does your lover need to hear you say: "I love you."

Thomas Carlyle wrote: "Under all speech that is good for anything lies a silence that is better." This is especially true of love.

Union is complete when awareness is complete, not otherwise. It occurs when the thinking mind is silent. Saying: "I love you" or anything else at such times would lessen the experience, disrupt love's flow.

* Does love make you vulnerable? (Yes. No.)

Does love make you vulnerable?

We associate love with weakness. The opposite is true.

Weakness and vulnerability stem from self-interest, from fearing loss, from wanting something for yourself. Love is selfless. In real love no self is there to be injured. Real love is strength.

* Is it exclusive? (Yes. No.)

Song lyrics say: "I love *only* you." Is your love exclusive?

Commitment is exclusive, but real love excludes no one. Like water from a hose, everyone receives love. If there is someone you do not love, your hose is clogged. In this way your love is diminished to the radiance of a star. The one you are committed to is also missing out.

- Is it conditional? (Yes. No.)

Would your love end if circumstances changed?

Would it end if the loved one changed?

If so it is conditional. Look for self-interest here.

- Does it feel like *your* love? (Yes. No.)

Does it feel like *your* love? Does loving feel like something you do that is under your control?

The real thing is not like this. Real love takes you by surprise. It is something you experience, not something turned on and off at will. If it feels like it is yours to control, you can probably do much better.

- Could it be just a beautiful concept? (Yes. No.)

Did you think-yourself-into love?

Are you lost in a dream or fantasy?

Confined to thoughts and dreams we miss reality. Love can easily be an illusion.

Real love arises from the union awareness creates. Without awareness love is not real. When it is manufactured by mind, love is an illusion.

- Rapture? Ecstasy? Bliss? (Yes. No.)

Do the words rapture, ecstasy, and bliss, mean little or nothing to you?

Real love is extra-ordinary and calls for extraordinary words.

- Misunderstanding? (Yes. No.)

Would you say that you "just do not understand" the one you love?

Real love is born of awareness. Awareness creates empathy. You feel what the loved one feels. In real love you would not be likely to say: "I just don't understand you."

- Do you run a "relationship program?" (Yes. No.)

Do you act out of love, or are you simply running a "relationship program?"

Running a program means acting out of concepts of what a relationship should be. The program specifies: "say the words; send the cards, remember to call," etc. Actions like these can easily exist in the absence of love. Running a program it is possible to miss the real thing and not even know it.

- Are you relating to a concept? (Yes. No.)

Are you relating to a concept of a loved one or to the reality.

Our mental habit is to relate to our concepts of others. We form concepts of people and get stuck in them for life. It sometimes happens that to Grandma, "Grandpa" is a tired old concept. Grandpa sees her in the same way. The little grand children, living in awareness, see two bright beacons of love, but Grandma and Grandpa see only their concepts of each other and without knowing it they relate to these.

Relating to concepts we miss the intimacy awareness creates. We can be holding hands and still be disconnected. The mental noise bars love.

- Do you blame unhappiness on inadequacy in a partner? (Yes. No.)

If you are unhappy, do you blame the unhappiness on some lack in your partner? Do you feel you need to be given more love?

Here self-interest wants to get (not give) love. This goes opposite the direction of the flow of the real thing.

- Are you unsure if it is love? (Yes. No.)

Are you unsure if you love someone?

Real love comes with deep awareness. Awareness knows for sure.

- Does love have a motive? (Yes. No.)

Do you love in order to be loved in return?

Do you love so as to have what others want or seem to have?

Any motive points to taking, and taking suggests an illusion of love. Real love has no motive any more than a rosebud has a motive for opening.

- Is it on and off? (Yes. No.)

Are you on and off, in and out of love?

Look deeper. Real love is eternal.

- ## Do you "give until it hurts?"

Do you give to your loved one "until it hurts?"

This expression shows our confusion; our self-interest agenda, our broken compass. It shows how blind we really are.

- ## Is the loved one taken for granted? (Yes. No.)

At parting, do you treat your loved one as if today's meeting might be your last?

This is true love's action. This is how it feels if you do not take the loved one for granted. If you do take the loved one for granted, outflow is not present.

- ## Are you still seeking happiness? (Yes. No.)

Are you still seeking happiness?

This is the most telling love test of all. When love is real the answer is emphatically no.

As Ram Dass said, in love "the human heart *goes out.*" This giving is happiness itself. That love and happiness are separate and distinct things is an accident of speech, an illusion created by words.

When love is real, pursuit of happiness ends. You turn around. You want for nothing. The self-interest program shuts down. Awareness is all-sufficing, and happiness comes free.

How Many "Yeses"?

"Yes" answers are as normal as low awareness. They are as common as is the illusion of love. All of us can be confused, even devoted seekers. "How can I find happiness," the seeker asks. "Help others...serve," says the Guru. He does, but does so in order to find happiness for himself. An unknowing taker can end up burnt out and depressed. It is possible to follow the self-interest agenda even in apparent giving.

"Yes" answers to the questions above confirm that the program is running. While it does there can be no love, no *unconditional* love that is, and unconditional love is the only kind that is real.

"Yeses" mean that more exists in you, inborn, unseen radiance that comes to life with awareness. With awareness, love outflows spontaneously and naturally. Awareness changes your direction, makes a giver of a taker. Danny Rubin's wonderful story *Groundhog Day* (Columbia Pictures, 1993) illustrates the turn around.

Running the Program: The *Groundhog Day* Story

A good illustration of the self-interest program we run is Phil's story. Phil, a TV weatherman goes to Punxsutawney, PA to report on Groundhog Day. He runs a taker program and follows it to the letter. Self-absorbed and superior, he calls himself "the talent," looks down on everyone to raise himself up, and looking down nothing good can enter his life. He hates the day, takes pleasure in nothing and can not wait to leave, but on waking next morning, Groundhog Day comes again. Next morning and on those that follow, the day continues to repeat. Endlessly it is Groundhog Day and he is stuck there.

What does Phil do?

He does what he always does, what most people do all the time. He pursues happiness. He does so through attempts at self-gratification. He sees his chance to have it all, to have everything his way and get what he wants. "No tomorrow means no hangovers, no consequences," he says, "I'm not living by *their* rules anymore." He gets what he wants and does as he pleases, overeating, drinking and having affairs. He collects big bags of money and has limitless opportunity for self-indulgence with no penalties. Yet no fulfillment comes.

Phil's pursuit of happiness brings the opposite of happiness. His life becomes want-in-a-holding-pattern; wanting something for himself. Again and again he tries to fill himself but registers empty. He has "boaters' two-foot-itis." (A fourteen-foot boat owner wants a sixteen-footer, but after getting that, an eighteen holds promise of happiness.) Phil assumes, as the program specifies, that when he gets all he wants things will be different. His circumstance affords him the chance to have it all. If Phil had a boat it could have been upsized to a fleet of giant yachts. With this comes a chance to learn the lesson our short lives miss: even "having it all," tomorrow will not be different.

The program says "attend to your own welfare, interest or advantage," and happiness will be just around the corner. *Groundhog Day* shows us that around the corner is another corner, and there is another after that. The program inevitably fails. We see Phil on a treadmill trying to overtake happiness, and each time he fails his need grows. The stronger his need to take, the less Phil has to give. Emptiness expands.

In time, Phil wants love. He sees it as something to take, and he tries to trick a good, kind woman into loving him by pretending to be the man of her dreams. She sees right through him. "I could never love anyone like you Phil because you'll never love anyone but yourself." Phil's answer is telling: "That's not true," he says. "I don't even *like* myself."

The more the program fails the more self-interest increases. Wanting more and more Phil has less and less to give. He cycles down until he reaches the point furthest from love, all-consuming self-interest, a weary, soul-aching depression from which even suicide is no escape. Tomorrow will not be different. The broken compass will not change its direction. His pain however great, does not serve as a wake-up call. This is why it takes Phil forever to change.

Going the Wrong Way

"The present is payday," as Master Deac says. Through self-interest, not only do we miss payday, *we pay*. Going contrary to our nature is the root cause of dis-ease.

It is better to give because to give is our nature. Going against the grain caused Phil friction, abrasion, splinters and snags, the pain we experience every day and see as normal.

Miss Benning's lesson illustrated how we act blindly running programs, persisting, whatever the outcome. It did not matter if the bread was torn or the lid was hit again and again needlessly. Actions can be futile and self-destructive and still programs run on, hurting ourselves and others. As in Phil's case, pain does not change our direction.

Our concept of a lone needy self makes others and the world *outside us* objects to exploit. We take from everywhere including earth's resources without giving back. We are repeat-offenders no matter how painful the consequences of our actions. Knowing something is wrong changes nothing when knowing is the noise of thinking in the absence of awareness. Concepts of "right" and "wrong" can help guide us, but they can not fix the broken compass. No concept can substitute for contact with reality, awareness of truth.

And so we learn from Phil that the problem of self-interest is deep seated and far reaching in consequences. We see too why a lifetime is not long enough to learn to love: life's most important lesson. Fortunately, the solution is simple.

The Solution: Awareness

The spiritual traditions have long recognized the problem of self-interest. Buddha taught that life is suffering caused by wants and cravings, "self" being their source. The traditions have been inclined to "kill the self." "Wield the sword of wisdom," says Zen, "and kill this self." ." From Islamic tradition comes the teaching: "In the death of the self lies the life of the heart (Iman Ja'far Al-Sadiq, eighth century)." "This rascal ego must be obliterated," says a Hindu text (Vivekananda, 1987, page 395). "Aim for true and perfect Annihilation" (of will) says Christian tradition. Enlightenment has been called "ego's great death," but the solution is simpler and easier than this. Trying to kill the self keeps you ensnared. Only become aware and self-interest vanishes like a cloud of vapor.

"Self" is a concept. It is no more than a thought. If you quiet the mind all thoughts quiet, including thoughts of self. Then the self-interest program shuts down. It is no longer needed because emptiness is filled by awareness. Your eyes open to beauty, your senses to pleasure, your mind to truth and your heart to love. You reside in a mansion of riches and out of the abundance, love flows naturally. *Quiet the mind.* The solution is that simple.

Phil's story shows us what has to be done. He did not need to kill the self to be liberated. Awareness freed his natural warmth and radiance. This freedom can be achieved in two ways. It can grow progressively from long term meditation practice. Thoughts of self can also vanish suddenly in an enlightenment breakthrough to full awareness. Toni Packer observed: "Truly seeing that the 'me' is nothing but a habitual mental construct is freeing beyond imagination."

Awareness overrides self-interest. It replaces the broken compass with a perfectly reliable direction finder: contact with reality. Without awareness it is impossible to love. With it, it is impossible not to. Then, with no pre-set agenda you go the right way. All it takes is awareness.

- ### Awareness is all it Takes
Happiness comes naturally to young children because they have awareness. Adults do what everyone else is doing and take a beating.

We do what everyone else is doing because we are thinking what everyone else is thinking. The noisy tenant is not an ally in the search for happiness. The mind reasons: "Having it all is the answer." But having it all does not even include having what it takes.

Pause a minute and picture "the guy who really knows how to live." What is he doing? Is it some form of self-gratification or self-indulgence? We assume this will fill our emptiness when only awareness can. *Awareness alone gratifies.*

Remember childhood car trips? "Are we there yet? Are we there yet?" As adults we are restless for the same reason. We are not there and never will be, going this route. We do not know how to live.

Some look to principles for solutions. Author Bill Elliott (1995) asked renowned spiritual leaders: "On what principles do you base your life?" Most listed principles. It surprised me because the lives of these persons appear to be spontaneous expressions of human nature. It seemed to me that these persons of wisdom do not base their lives on principles any more than a flower bases its fragrance on principles. Principles come after the fact.

Fourth Master MoKow said actions should come "out of truth" (consistent with reality) not out of words in books. Persons of wisdom *know how to live* because they abide in the love and goodness born of awareness.

At the height of his career football player Chris Spielman left his multi-million dollar job as linebacker for the Buffalo Bills to help his wife through breast cancer. People were shocked. A reporter interviewing Spielman said: "It must have been a very tough decision." Spielman answered: "No. It was easy. I did it out of human nature." His wife recovered and looking back he says it was the best year of his life. What steered Spielman? Awareness.

Joan Tollifson (1992) said: "Love is like gravity. It draws you to the center." At the center is your true nature. There, awareness overrides self-interest. Right choices are not tough decisions. Instead actions arise spontaneously out of human nature.

How do you get centered there? Moral principles can be undermined without your knowing it. Intending to love (as I did with the hairdresser) can fool us too. Helping and serving can be illusions of giving. "He who likes to take," as the proverb says, "does not like to give." Only awareness lets you be what you are; lets you be love.

Aristotle said: "Love is life's meaning and purpose, the whole aim and end of human existence." Learning to love is life's main lesson. Confusion and illusion make it all but impossible to learn.

As we will see later, awareness lets you *be* love, and when you are, actions that bring happiness flow as freely as a Karate man's moves when he is not confused about what he is.

> ' *Right' and the 'wrong' at once become apparent all by themselves* (Chuang Tzu, in Merton, 1965, page 101).

An Indian fable tells of a Prince stolen in infancy by a gang of thieves. Raised in poverty with vagabonds he never knew what he was, never knew the noble origin that could have freed him from misery. You are that Prince and you can return to your noble origin. Awareness takes you home.

CHAPTER SIX
THE FEEDBACK METHOD

Attention! Attention! Attention!
Zen Sage

I visited a maze as a child. It was in a local state park. From the park entrance high on a hill you could see the whole maze at once. It covered an acre with eight-foot hedges and corridors several feet wide. What struck me most about the maze however, was the view from inside. Inside the maze, wherever I stood I saw two hedges, one on each side; that was all. Inside there was no sense of a maze, and with no sense of a maze, there was no indication of being lost.

The mind is like this. We are always inside a maze of thoughts. Our wants and worries are high walls we can not see beyond. That is why we do not realize we are lost.

This chapter holds the solution. Unlike other paths to liberation, the method taught here does not wander the corridors of mind looking for an exit. It lifts clean out.

Read all instructions before beginning. To start, you will need a disc for focusing attention.

-   Setting up for the Feedback Method
To make a basic focusing disc, trace a circle the size of a quarter or a bit larger on a sheet of white paper. Cut it out. Put a black dot, split-pea size, in the center. This bull's eye is your focus point. Now, position the disc.

Positioning the Disc
Place the disc on the floor several feet in front of you as in Figure 1 (page 72). Sit with your eyes closed a minute; then open them.

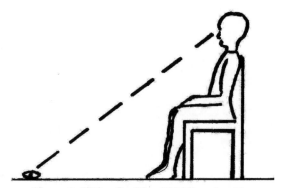

Figure 1: Sitting Position "Sit Like a Lord"

Is your gaze centered? If not, reposition the disc to where your eyes rest naturally, downcast at about a forty-five degree angle. Trust instinct to get placement right. When it is right it feels right. If it is off even by an inch, you will not feel comfortable. Now for sitting the position.

<u>Sit Like A Lord</u>

Erect posture is vital. If your body is slumped and sluggish, your mind will be too.

Use a straight back chair. Sit with your buttocks as far back in the chair as possible, your back gently arched. As illustrated in Figure 1, sit like a Lord.

The floor, another option, has a solid, down to business feel. Use a mat or carpet. Kneel and then sit, resting your weight on a cushion between your legs. Whether using a chair or the floor, be comfortable. Only then does it feel like you could sit forever. That is how it should feel.

<u>Focus Attention</u>

Focus on the bull's eye and visual distortions will appear. When your mind wanders your eyes wander and distortions end. Distortions are feedback. They are proof of attention.

Avoid eye strain. Think of your eyes as windows. Open windows let air in freely. The disc will enter your eyes just as easily. A passive gaze is all it takes. This is not done with the eyes but with the heart and soul.

- ### How to use Feedback

Focus on the bull's eye with a gentle gaze. When distortions appear, attend to them. A vise grip is not necessary. Hold the distortion the way a mother holds a newborn baby: you are at ease yet nothing can tear you away.

What to Expect?

What can you expect to see?

Feedback signals vary widely according to degree and duration of attention and the disc used. Once in a while feedback is a fine detail or a color more vibrant than normally seen. Most of the time however, feedback is distortion like this:

- Halos of light.
- Dark circles around the disc.
- Double images (two discs appear).
- The bull's eye or part of the disc disappears.

If the disc rests on a braided rug or colorful tile, feedback puts on quite a show, but do not expect fireworks. Most feedback signals will be slight and brief.

Now for some Dos and Don'ts.

Feedback Method Dos and Don'ts

- **Do Be All There**. Typically we are half there; daydreaming while driving, dozing while watching TV. When you sit down to focus attention, engage your whole being. Be *all* there.

- **Don't Strain Your Eyes**. Don't strain or stare at the disc. Don't give it a hard look. Your gaze should be relaxed and easy, but steadfast.

- **Do *Let it* Happen**. Feedback comes automatically so just let it happen.

- **Don't Expect Fireworks**. Don't expect fireworks. You don't need them.

- <u>Don't Forget Feedback Means Attention</u>. Feedback means you are paying attention and attention is what you are here for.

These are the basics. Aim for a half hour practice session daily. Do no less than fifteen minutes per session. If you have only seconds of feedback, that is okay. Each second is potent. Stay with this exercise until the Self-tests tell you to move on.

Problem File: Questions and Answers

Questions may arise as you go along. Here are some answers.

Is "A" Still With You?
While focusing you may find yourself repeating "A" from Exercise One. Let "A" come if it wants to but when it stops let it go. You do not need it now.

Practice not Relaxed?
This exercise should feel energetic and alert (not collapsed like meditation often does). You will however, feel relaxed when you finish your session.

Painful Sitting?
Attention is the aim here. Pain disrupts attention. Pain problems must be addressed.

Poor posture is a common cause of pain. Babies sit with perfect posture, backs straight, heads aligned with hips. Lacking motor skills to compensate for being off kilter, they have to sit straight or fall over. Adults do sit out of kilter, causing strain, fatigue and pain.

To improve posture, try this. Stand and imagine a two-liter bottle in the air above your head. Extend your arms out to the sides and reach up. Take hold of the bottle with both hands and lower it slowly onto your head. Feel the rib cage lift and expand. This is how good posture feels.

To help achieve good posture:
- Use props. A rolled towel at the small of your back can help.
- Place pads or pillows at stress points.
- The slightest head tilt causes strain. Be sure only your eyes are downcast.

- If chronic back pain keeps you from sitting upright, lie down and focus on a point on the ceiling, but take care to avoid drowsiness.

Do whatever it takes to stop pain from disrupting attention.

Distracting Thoughts?

Meditation tradition offers this advice on handling distracting thoughts.

Imagine you are in a railway terminal. Trains, like thoughts, are coming and going in all directions. They will carry you away, but only if you board.

If you do board, you will go where the train is going and you may be carried away.

Stay at attention however and no train will come. Feedback means attention so hold on to feedback. If you lose it, return to attention as soon as you see you are being carried away.

Bad Mood? No Test of Success.

Are you in a bad mood after practicing?

Now and then you might feel impatient or irritable after a session, but passing moods, even good ones, are no test of success. Feedback is the measure of a session. If feedback is present, sooner or later results will be too.

Is a Session without Feedback Wasted?

You may have practice sessions without feedback. Are these sessions a waste of time?

Think of it this way. When working out, if you tried to lift a weight you could not budge, you might think you accomplished nothing. The resistance you exerted however was still useful exercise. The same applies here. Effort counts, so no session is wasted.

In horseshoes a ringer wins, but close is good too. Not all sessions will be ringers but know the value of getting close. Be aware, as Master Deac teaches, that no time is wasted when something is learned. Learn what it takes to score a ringer tomorrow.

Self-analysis?

Awareness brings insight, but this is not self-analysis.

The aim here is getting out of the maze, not going deeper in. Be *aware now* and you will not need analysis. Just clear your head.

Doubting Progress?

If you are putting time in and doubting progress, consider this.

Suppose you owned a gym full of body building equipment and a friend asked to use it. If your friend came back and said: "It didn't work," you would know that *he* had not worked.

The instructions here are keys to the gym. Attention pumps iron; awareness is the muscle it builds. To progress you have to workout. You can fail to do this exercise, but this exercise can not fail you. Expect to get out of it exactly what you put in.

Want to Skip Ahead?

You may want to go straight to advanced practice. Let me explain why you should not.

Psychologists study skill learning in animals. In one experiment, a mouse is placed in the start position of a puzzle box. It explores the maze and finds food at the exit. With repeated trials the skill of maze running is learned and the mouse goes quickly from start to finish.

Attention is a skill, and learning it is something like what the mouse does. If you do not know where you are going or what is around the corner, you can not run full speed. To be skilled at getting feedback is to be skilled at paying attention. Develop the skill. Then you can go top speed to the goal.

Does "Trying" Get in your Way?

Is a strain of "trying" taking energy away from your session?

This problem will decrease as your practice skill grows. If you like however, when you sit down to practice, say to yourself: "Let God do it." See what happens.

What if you Stop?

What happens if you stop practicing?

You might say practice is a power tool that clears a path to your mansion. Each time you go through your cutting tool gets sharper and your passage easier. After many times through, reaching greater awareness is effortless. Your way is clear.

Stop practicing however and your power tool dulls. You will feel resistance, and resistance can stop you.

If resistance stops you, go back to the beginning and start again. Lie down and repeat "A". Starting again will ease you back into it. Soon you will return to the practice level where you left off. And if you do stop, whatever stops you, remember this: all things pass, including impasses.

Intermediate Self-tests

I was biking fast around a sharp turn. A fallen limb lay in my path. In a split second I maneuvered around it. I gave myself an "A" for awareness.

Then straight ahead in my path I saw a bright orange salamander. It lay dead in my track, run over on my first lap of the trail. It stood out like a neon sign against dark earth, yet I had not seen it. I learned a sad lesson here. Never score yourself an "A" without testing your awareness. The Self-tests serve this purpose.

Without Self-tests we are not able to gauge awareness. Self-tests let you know where you stand. Fifty-one are provided here measuring attention, awareness and growth of practice skill. As before, ration them.

Those with "I" indicate imagery. If you have good imagery, these are especially for you.

Those with asterisks (*) are feedback exercises that confirm attention just as work with the disc does. These alternate exercises will help keep your practice fresh and interesting. (For easy access these alternate exercises are listed in the Appendix, page 217.)

Self-test 32: Looking for Results?

When you sit down to practice are you looking for results?

Having one eye on the disc and one eye on results divides attention. Instead of looking for results, aim for attention for the sake of attention.

Self-test 33: A Posture Check.

When you sit down to practice do you collapse into a chair?

Be sure your body is engaged as well as your mind. Try this posture test. Open your hand fully, little finger and thumb as far apart as possible. Sit with the tip of the little finger on your navel. How high on your chest does your thumb reach?

Now place your thumb under your breastbone (feel the notch) and put your little finger on your navel. Open your hand fully, lifting the rib cage until your open hand fits. Note the feeling of good posture.

Self-test 34: Disappearing Disc. *

With good attention the whole disc can disappear. It will reappear when your mind wanders. This happens more easily in dim light. Try it both ways.

Self-test 35: Daydreaming?—A Motivation Test.

How much practice time do you spend daydreaming?

If you daydream it is for one reason only, because *you want to.* Daydreaming means you want to linger in the maze more than you want to get free.

Daydreaming is likely to be a motivation problem. Get help from Chapter Nine (How To Stay Motivated, page 117).

Self-test 36: Seeing what is There. (I) *

Picture a cloudy sky.

Do you see a still shot like a photographic image?

Looking at the sky we tend to see still shots, but that is not what is there. Clouds are *never* still. The average life of a cloud is less than ten minutes.

Go out on a cloudy day and see if you can see what is before your eyes. Make this your practice session. Use cloud movement as feedback. **Seeing continuous movement proves continuous attention.**

At first you will see only the cloud you are focusing on move. Deeper awareness sees the whole sky's motion. Full awareness sees a rare sight as clouds come into existence out of nothing. What do you see? Where do you stand in terms of awareness?

Self-test 37: Beyond Distraction?

When practicing, are you easily distracted? If a car passes do you look up to see it? If others are talking, do you wonder what they are saying?

The more skilled your practice, the less such distraction occurs. In time you will be beyond distraction.

Self-test 38: The "It" That Breathes.

Some meditators practice "It breathes." With each inhalation "It breathes" is silently voiced. At first the words make no sense. They conflict with a concept that "I breathe." After a while however, the meditator feels "It" breathing with no help at all from "I."

Try it. Are you aware that "It breathes?"

Keep going until "I breathe" seems like empty nonsense.

Self-test 39: In Sync with the Sun? *

For today's exercise sit by a sunny window. Focus on the shadow, the border of sun and shade on the floor. Do not try to accomplish anything, just attend to the line. Can you see it move?

At first the line might tremble. Dark and light borders may appear along it. Such distortions confirm attention and serve as feedback.

Sustained attention however sees the smooth steady movement of the line. Can you get in sync with the sun? Hold that line.

Self-test 40: Are You Seeing Spots?

Next time you see a movie see if you notice the round spots that flash periodically at the corners of the screen. These spots signal projectionists to switch reels and are most easily seen in old, black-and-white films where frames move slowly. If you can not see these spots, you can not see what is before your eyes.

In time you will see them and once you do you will be amazed you ever missed them. You will see how blind, how lost in thought we actually are.

Self-test 41: Can you Change Direction?

When you enter a group, is your attention on you? How do I look? Will they accept me? Will they like me? What can I gain here?

If you are seeing yourself in it, turn this around. Next time you enter a group repeat silently: "Not for me...for them. Not for me...*for them.*" Say it on your way there and as you enter.

Did you get past self-interest? How did it feel?

Living your true nature always feels better than running the taker program. "Help your brother's boat across and lo, you have reached the other shore."

Self-test 42: Everything is Relative.

Let someone else drive and try this.

Riding along, can you see the car as still and the road moving?

This is a test of awareness. Deep awareness sees that everything is relative.

Self-test 43: Entering the Moment?

Are you trying to enter the present moment?

With more awareness you will not be. To live in the present is to live in eternity.

Self-test 44: An Attention Walk. *

Take a walk and attend to your feet. Center yourself in the sensations. Feel movement; contact with the ground; the texture of your socks, whatever you sense. When your mind drifts, come back to your feet.

After your walk check what you saw or heard that you normally miss. Did you hear sounds like rustling leaves or perhaps your footsteps? Awareness of these sights and sounds confirms attention. Take another attention walk tomorrow.

Self-test 45: More Painful to Hear?

A prominent newscaster wore a pleasant smile as he said: "one thousand dead in flooding." He was clearly out of contact with reality.

As awareness grows, you may find the nightly news more painful to hear. If so you are coming into contact with reality. A temporary "news fast," as Dr. Andrew Weil suggests, might be advised.

Self-test 46: Free like Sisyphus?

Sisyphus, a character in Greek mythology, was condemned by the Gods to roll a boulder up Mt. Olympus for all eternity. When he reached the peak, the boulder rolled back to the bottom where he started again. His fate imprisoned him. One day however, he came to awareness. He felt the sun on his face; the strain of his sinews; the breeze on his moist back, and he was set free.

Do you feel imprisoned in a fate of commuting to work, filing papers, changing diapers, tending shop? These only seem to imprison you. Your concept is your prison. When you "work" in a garden, as my little one taught me, you do some unnecessary suffering. Can you free yourself as Sisyphus did: with awareness.

Self-test 47: Drugs or Alcohol?

Do you crave drugs or alcohol?

If so you are pleasure-impaired. When pleasure is low you want to get high.

The more aware you become, the less pleasure-impaired you will be. When fully aware, life gratifies fully, being alive is a natural high and alcohol feels like the depressant it is. It actually takes the edge off your happiness.

Self-test 48: Attention Span—Going Up? (I)

Test your attention span. Close your eyes and imagine standing at the top of a down escalator. Picture the moving steps and handrails. Step on, hold the rails, and descend slowly to the landing. Keep your hands on the rails. If you let go, you have wandered off.

Can you go one flight without breaking concentration?

If so, try two.

Self-test 49: Does Wasting Hurt?

Do you use a big sheet of paper to write a short note?

Do you throw away bottles you could recycle?

Do you leave lights on when you leave a room?

Making one cup of tea, do you heat a whole pot of water?

As awareness grows such habits may change. In perfect union with nature, wasting feels like opening a vein. Ask yourself: Does wasting hurt?

Self-test 50: Staying on Course?

Do you stay on course in practice sessions?

I found a role model for staying on course, a cormorant feeding at the ocean in Maine. Moving like a sleek black bullet, it never slowed, wavered or changed direction. Ships in its way were circumvented with wide arcs so graceful it seemed no impediment existed.

I like to practice like this: go straight, maintain my speed and let nothing change my direction. On course in this way, you sustain attention and stretches of feedback lengthen.

Self-test 51: "Every Minute Zen?"

A Zen student left his umbrella and clogs in the hall before entering. The Master asked: "On which side of your clogs is your umbrella?" The student could not answer.

Think back to the last person you interacted with, a family member or co-worker. Do you recall what he or she wore? What about eye color, glasses, expression, voice?

Recalling details points to "every minute Zen:" continuous awareness.

Self-test 52: Make a Sandwich.

Imagine a frog on a lily pad thinking: "Next fly that comes, I'm going for it." Imagine a dog carrying a bone thinking: "I'll take this home now and chew it later." Such talk seems absurd compared to just doing it, but such talk is exactly what we fill our lives with.

We make a sandwich at noon preoccupied with needless thoughts of "making a sandwich in order to have it for lunch." We miss ninety-five percent of the sandwich making experience, the bread's softness, the jam's glistening color and sweet fragrance. Slaves to a concept, we run a "sandwich program" that blinds us to limitless possibilities. That is why it is no fun making a sandwich and why it is always the same old thing.

Next lunchtime, be silent. Taste life.

Self-test 53: The Minute Hand. *

For today's session, focus on the minute hand of a clock (preferably one without a second hand). Make the minute hand your bull's eye. With good attention you will see it move. This movement is feedback.

Backward jerks are usually seen first. These indicate good attention, but seeing a smooth sweep is best. A smooth sweep means continuous attention.

Self-test 54: A Problem Person? (I)

Think of a problem person in your life, someone you dislike or resent. In imagination, hold that person's head in your hands and gaze into his/her eyes.

Are you able to do this?

With growing awareness you will be. Understanding comes with awareness, and understanding brings the acceptance necessary for love.

Self-test 55: Human Tuning Fork?

Are you distressed with someone who is distressed; tense with someone tense; sad with an unhappy person?

This is the human tuning fork phase in growth of awareness. It ends when the barrier to love's outflow is gone. Then someone in distress becomes your chance for happiness.

Self-test 56: Touch A Tree.

A man attempting suicide went over Niagara Falls and survived. Afterward he said he had seen "strangely beautiful sunlight" through the water. Why did he see beauty? Why was it "strange?"

A crisis summons full attention. At that moment he was not half-there. He saw reality more clearly than ever, and so it was something strange and new to him.

Have you seen reality? Repeat: "Touch a tree" from Chapter Two (Self-test 24). Does the tree touch you back now? Does it touch your heart? Can you see why you had to be told: "Don't touch!" so often as a child? (Note your experience. We will return to this later.)

Self-test 57: Do you have a Match? (I)

Take a moment to picture yourself happy, deeply, lastingly happy. Get the whole picture: the place you are in, who you are with, what you are doing, how it feels.

Now form another image. Picture yourself successful. Get the whole picture. Imagine the place you are in, who you are with, what you are doing, how it feels.

Do your happy and successful images match?

As awareness grows, these images will come to agree more and more. When fully aware you will have one perfect match.

Self-test 58: Is Acceptance Growing?

At Walden Pond, Thoreau did not condemn the rain that ruined his bean crop. He knew it would make the upper grasses thrive and benefit him later. A big picture shows perfect balance.

Master Deac teaches: "What is is. What is must be. What is should be."

Seeing "what is" means contact with reality.

Seeing why things "must be" is awareness of cause and effect.

Seeing why things "should be" is grasping a big picture. This comes with deepest awareness.

Is your picture getting bigger as Thoreau's did? Is your acceptance growing?

Self-test 59: Do You Want To Practice?

Do you want to practice?

Wanting to means good work. When you are doing your best work you will want to practice all the time.

Self-test 60: Thinking Things Through?

When having a problem with your boss, your spouse or child, should you take time to think things through?

Conventional wisdom says you should. There is however, deeper wisdom. Thinking will not cure blindness, and blindness is very likely to be the cause of your problem. Take some time to *stop thinking*. Allow thoughts to settle and solutions to appear.

Self-test 61: "Happy Jolts?"

You may experience sudden unaccountable joy, "happy jolts" as one student called them. I saw these surges of happiness in my baby. They are caused by breakthroughs to awareness.

If you experience a happy jolt, take note of what you are aware of. You will probably discover something you have been missing, something that was there all along.

Self-test 62: Are you "Giving" or "Taking?"

Suppose you gave someone a gift that was not appreciated. This could upset you, but why? The answer may be that you were *taking*, not giving.

When giving, your heart goes out. You feel pain for the unhappy receiver.

When taking, in this circumstance, you feel pain for yourself.

Signs of taking are: "Will my gift be remembered? Will my good taste impress him? Will I get something in return?"

Signs of true giving are compassion, care, warmth, a sympathetic ear, cooperative spirit, undivided attention and pure joy. These outflow naturally when awareness directs your course.

Self-test 63: Wonder and Awe?

Through a portal of silence, as awareness deepens, a new world enters. You may experience something you have missed since childhood. It is the state where "a leaf of grass is no less than the journey work of the stars...a mouse is miracle enough to stagger sextillions of infidels (Whitman)." It is awe and wonder.

Have you felt awe and wonder?

Self-test 64: Awareness Override?

Have you had an awareness override?

Here is an example of what I mean. An elderly neighbor called one morning asking me to come over. I grumbled to myself: "I can't go. I have work to do. My time is important." Self-interest made lots of noise, but it was only noise; nothing more. In the midst of the noise I walked out the door going to my neighbor's aid.

I had an awareness override. I was too aware to do the wrong thing. (Entering my neighbor's kitchen I saw a bright bouquet of flowers on the table. I knew I was being guided. She had called me down to give me these.)

Deep down we always know the right thing to do. The small voice of conscience is small only because it is drowned by the noise of thinking, the noise of self-interest. As the noise quiets, increasingly awareness directs your course. As Chris Spielman showed us in Chapter Five, acting "out of human nature" creates awareness overrides.

Self-test 65: Watch the Pot.

Next time you boil water, watch the pot. If it never boils and you climb the walls you are far from awareness. When aware, a watched pot engrosses completely and boils too soon.

Self-test 66: Less Fantasy?

Are you having fewer daydreams; less fantasy?

A song lyric says: "Fantasy will set you free," but this is not so. Daydreams may feel like escape, but you are still living in your head.

Master Choe said: "Most people are already dead." When you come to life you will not want to escape. Instead you will want greater union; more presence in the vibrant heart of reality. Awareness is more gratifying than any possible thought.

Self-test 67: Future Planning?

Reflect a minute. Five years from now, where do you want to be?

One answer gets a perfect score: in your *right mind.*

In Dickens' classic, the enlightened Scrooge says: "I don't deserve to be so happy. I just can't help it." Your practice takes you in the direction of happiness, just where you want to be.

Self-test 68: A Question from Karate dō.

You are on a journey you have prepared for with adequate provisions. You meet a traveler along the way who has not prepared for his journey and has run out of supplies. Master Deac asks: "Should you give him some of yours?"

"No" is the answer. If you give him your provisions you will run short and neither of you will make it. You will also prevent him from learning a vital lesson. He is his own responsibility. You are yours.

Self-test 69: Retest your SQ.

Eckart Tolle (2001) says "we are insane." This is literally true. To lose awareness is to lose contact with reality, and we are far less aware (less sane) than we think.

How far are we from perfect sanity? As far as we are from full awareness.

The Feedback Method makes it possible to measure this distance as never before. With it you can find out *how sane you are.*

Feedback measures your capacity to see what is before your eyes. It gauges your contact with reality. The more aware you are, the more sane you are.

SQs rise with ability to sustain attention. Retake Chapter Two Self-tests and see what has changed.

Self-test 70: Do you need to be Entertained?

Remember the baby at Fourth of July fireworks. Entranced by a jingling key chain she had no need to be entertained. The rest of the family did, yet they missed most of the pleasure. They looked up without seeing all that was there.

The father was blinded by tax dollars going up in flames: "This one cost a bundle...That one cost a fortune." The boys labeled and judged: "A red one...A blue one...This one's biggest...no that one!" Their faces did not glow like the baby's.

Do you still need to be entertained? The need lessens as awareness grows.

Self-test 71: Are You Finding Guidance?

Think of some current trouble in your life. Ask yourself: "If this were the *best* thing that could possibly happen to me, how could I benefit?"

Awareness sees silver linings in darkest clouds. When awareness is high, the search for guidance ends. With enough awareness (as the awareness exercise in Chapter Seven shows), troubles can be the best thing that could possibly happen to you.

Self-test 72: Cleaning Your Attic. (I)

Think of your mind as an attic. Walk up the back stairs and enter. Looking around you see clutter and no open space. Now clean your attic.

Place a dumpster in the center and clear away everything. Throw out petty things and big ones. Get rid of mistakes your parents made that hurt you and those you made that hurt yourself. Throw out victories and defeats, all you took to heart and kept there. Throw out good intentions with bad, broken and kept promises. Get rid of blame and shame...all the reasons you ever had for hating yourself. Go into dark corners, haul out the goblins and get rid of them too. Check to see that you have it all. Then close the dumpster. Look around and see clear in all directions.

Now return to the dumpster and lift the lid. *What is inside?*

If you answered "nothing," take a bow. It was all phantoms, the stuff of dreams. No matter what you are storing or how long it has been there, all of it can be cleared away to nothing. Entry into present reality sets you free.

Self-test 73: More Spontaneous Lately?

I had a three-year old Karate student who continuously invented ways to have more fun. He would step out of range, for instance, instead of standing still and learning to block. He had awareness of endless possibilities. It showed in spontaneous action.

"Judge quickly but not verbally," taught Master Choe. Non-verbal judgment is based on awareness where thoughts are "fluid," not solid. Awareness keeps concepts fluid, allowing spontaneous thought and action.

Are your conceptual traps loosening? Are you more spontaneous lately?

Self-test 74: Can You Laugh at Yourself?

Can you laugh at yourself?

If so, you know how good it feels. It feels good because it is a taste of liberation. It springs the self-concept trap. It proves the concept has no power over you. You laugh as if "self" were nothing, which truly it is.

In the words of a Christian mystic: "I am as vast as God. Nothing in the world O Miracle!—can shut me up in myself." This is how free you can feel.

Self-test 75: Why the Broom?

An eager student and a renowned Zen Master lived together in the woods. The student did his chores, gathering firewood and cooking, but was frustrated at receiving no instruction. All the Master did was sneak up from behind and hit him with a broom.

The student *was* receiving instruction. Can you tell what it was?

He was being taught to attend (lest he get hit). He was being trained in awareness.

Self-test 76: A Post-Test.

Complete this sentence. Three reasons why I am happy are:

1.

2.

3.

This was a trick question. Real happiness needs no reason. It comes free.

Are you experiencing the happiness that comes free?

Self-test 77: Breaking Cycles.

The boss yells at a worker who goes home and hollers at his wife. His wife gets angry with the son and the son kicks the dog. In the same way someone abused in childhood becomes an abuser. Someone abandoned abandons. The cheated becomes a cheat.

Are you trapped in such a cycle, passing on a legacy of pain?

Your practice can break such cycles. Longfellow wrote: "If we could read the secret history of our enemies, we'd find in each man's life sorrow and suffering enough to disarm all hostility." Awareness brings the understanding needed to forgive. This breaks the cycle. If you are a prisoner of your past, you are your own jailer. Awareness will set you free.

Self-test 78: Could you be Happy in Prison?

Imagine yourself imprisoned somewhere, given food and shelter, but not allowed to leave. Could you be happy?

If you said "no," look deeper. Even in prison you can be free.

Self-test 79: Discovering What You Are?

Picture yourself next to a skyscraper.

Now picture yourself amid block after block of them.

Now compare yourself to the size of the earth.

Now see yourself relative to the million times more massive sun where the earth itself is like a bump on its surface.

"I" can get very small. Does this trouble you? If so it has to do with a concept of self, with "who" you think you are.

People ask: "What is your baby's name?" No one asks: "*Who* is your baby?" "Who" is a concept that comes in later years. Free of the "who," you know fully what you are. When you do, the "who," very small by comparison, will not trouble you again.

Self-test 80: Finding Purpose in Pain?

Dr. Bernie Siegel says "life is a labor pain in which you give birth to yourself." Look back. Can you find purpose in pain? Ask: "Had it not been for the pain, I would not have _____."

Did pain lead you to awareness?

Were you running a toxic self-interest program?

Was there a turn around that left you corrected and balanced?

If you are in emotional pain now, can you see how awareness would end it?

Can you see how awareness might lead to love?

Think of feedback as a safety line. Take hold and pull yourself to safety. Pull yourself into mental balance. Pull yourself into awareness.

Self-test 81: Seeing Through Concepts?

You have seen how we are trapped in concepts of "age," "mind and body," of "who" we are, etc. Such concepts blind us to truth. Can you see through concepts?

Consider "bullying?" When this word is applied, brutal acts can be made to appear as innocent as "boys being boys." Can you see through the mask? With awareness you will.

Self-test 82: Vulnerability or Strength?

A Love Test (Chapter Five, page 61) asked if you associate love with vulnerability. Ask again: does love put you at risk?

As you grow in awareness, capacity for love grows too, and love, as we will see later, is power. Where once you saw vulnerability, you will find strength.

Self-test 83: What to do when Doubtful?

At any practice level you can be doubtful, pessimistic, discouraged. What will you do when you doubt you can succeed?

Action not words is the answer. You may not know it but you can burn through doubt and discouragement the way morning sun burns off a fog. With the Feedback Method you can sit down empty and get up full.

Sitting down to practice discouraged is like taking off in a plane on a cloudy day. However dark it is on the ground, keep going and you will soar through the clouds to brilliant sunlight.

Have you experienced this? Do you know you can sit down empty and get up full? Have you discovered the power of action not words? If so, you are ready for advanced practice.

Summing Up

Long ago, people seeking wisdom sent a representative to a sage for words to live by. The Master took a pen and wrote one word: "Attention."

The man asked: "Is that all? Won't you write a few more words?"

The Master took up the pen again and wrote "Attention. Attention."

This did not satisfy the man: "I don't see much depth or subtlety in what you have written."

The Master wrote again, this time three times: "Attention! Attention! Attention!"

Then the man protested: "After all, what does this word 'Attention' mean?"

"Attention," the master replied, "means *Attention*!"

The instruction in this chapter could be summed up in a single word. From beginner to advanced practice the same holds true. To restore awareness, attention is all you need.

CHAPTER SEVEN
HOW TO USE AND PREVENT PAIN

The purpose of incarnation on this earth is to correct and balance oneself.
T. L. Vaswani

W hat you need to know: Pain is a call to awareness. Answer the call and you will find guidance. If awareness is maintained, prevention of pain is possible.

They say desire for happiness is a homing instinct to perfection. Aversion to pain is too. Pain is a homing instinct to perfection because it calls us to awareness. When we answer the call, pain's purpose is served. That purpose is guidance.

This chapter can help you find guidance in life's pain. It has three parts.

First it offers tips on using pain.

Next come exercises designed to help broaden awareness.

Finally it explores the idea of the higher standard of sanity that awareness affords, and the possibility of prevention of pain. We start with tips on using pain.

Tips on Using Pain

As Chapter Four showed, we miss pain's call to awareness. This is why most of life's pain is meaningless suffering. If you answer the call however, there need be no meaningless suffering in your life.

First and foremost, to use pain well, stick to action not words. Let life's pain move you to practice.

• Let Pain Move You to Practice

Pain shouts: "This is urgent! Nothing is more so." This demands attention. Answer the call to awareness. Let pain serve its purpose. Let it move you to practice.

- ## A Rock-bottom Feeling? Don't be fooled!

Even if you are practicing at the advanced level, life's pain can make you feel you have gotten nowhere. Do not let this feeling fool you. It is like feeling broke, forgetting you have a big bank account; like the Karate man forgetting what he was.

Awareness accelerates growth, and fundamental change, as Master Deac teaches, is permanent. Every practice minute pays off and if you see no gain now you will later.

- ## Listen to your Body

As Chapter Four suggested, your body can serve as a guidance system. Awareness of early-warning body signals can help prevent bigger problems from developing. Watch for warnings in "stop signs."

"Stop Signs"

Listen to your body's subtle signals of dis-ease. If you respond to whispers the body will not have to shout. Let the whispers serve as "stop signs," warnings usually missed.

Take headaches, for instance. We say: "I was feeling fine this morning, then suddenly this awful headache." Headaches seem to come out of nowhere, but they do not. Even "sudden twitches" do not come out of nowhere. They seem sudden only because we are unaware of the tension buildup preceding them.

Headaches need not take us by surprise. They are preceded by small signals or stop signs. These might include restlessness; dry mouth; forgetfulness; light-headedness; trouble sleeping; sweaty palms; clenching or grinding of teeth; cracking voice; tunnel vision; butterflies in the stomach; stutter; stammer; muscle twitches, etc. As you grow in awareness, you may notice these more. You might notice, for instance, neck stiffness, irritability or cold hands before a headache.

These signals are barometers of imbalance. They say: "Act now or pay later! " Become aware of them. Make a list and react to them as you would to a tack in the shoe. Make them "stop signs." Restore awareness and you restore balance that can avert bigger problems later. "Aware presence," said Master Choe, "will save your life and it will save your soul."

- Use *all* your pain

Meaningless suffering need not be part of your life. Assume that what is must be and should be, and let awareness find purpose in pain.

All pain can serve as guidance. If you stub a toe or bend a fender, do not dismiss it as an accident. Bending a fender should tell you something important about your state of awareness. When you stub your toe ask "Why wasn't I aware?" The answer will open your eyes. Use *all* your pain.

- Use the pain of others too

Use the pain of others too. Let it open your heart, but remember, your life is not about fixing the world's pain. The world's pain, if it leads you to greater compassion, helps fix you.

Master Deac says: "Never put ointment on a wound you did not inflict." Everyone needs to make mistakes and learn his own lessons. Learn yours and ultimately the whole world will benefit.

- Watch what you are doing

My little one sometimes lost her sweet temper. Afterward I noticed that she was likely to hurt herself or accidentally break a toy. I told her these things were not accidents. It was her guardian angel saying: "Watch what you are doing. See what brings pain."

As adults, through low awareness, we do not watch what we are doing. Rarely do we see what brings pain. That is why, as in Phil's case, it takes forever for us to change.

In the end Phil's life changed because he changed. He let go of self-interest, stopped trying to change circumstances and changed himself. His pain ended when he stopped running the program and lived spontaneously according to his nature. This opened his eyes to beauty, his senses to pleasure, his mind to truth and his heart to love. He became a giver and a non-taker. He had the "helper's high" that goes with outflow: the happiness that comes free.

Groundhog Day shows us that a lifetime of running programs is not long enough to turn us around. Suppose an angel had whispered in his ear: "Watch what you are doing. See what brings pain." Would it have taken Phil forever to change?

- Expect more from the Feedback Method

A man mentioned in Chapter One meditated faithfully for many years and saw little benefit. Unlike you he lacked the advantage of feedback. You have a self-sharpening power tool he lacked, and you can expect more.

Chapters Eight, Nine and Ten will help improve your practice. Use them to grab hold of feedback and pull yourself to safety. Pull yourself into the all-sufficing state, the state that is itself the remedy. Pull yourself into awareness.

Now for some help with broadening awareness.

Awareness Exercises

The broader your awareness the more guidance you will derive from pain. The following exercises help broaden awareness. Awareness Exercise One helps you find meaning and purpose in pain.

Awareness Exercise One: Finding Meaning and Purpose in Pain

Use this exercise to broaden your awareness. Take some time and put yourself into it.

Think of yourself as the *only real person*. Imagine you are real and everyone else is a phantom. All of these phantoms and all your life circumstances exist to guide you. Life's drama plays for your benefit alone.

Bring to mind key people in your life. Helpful and problem people are equally your guides. Painful problems with a boss, spouse or child position you to learn and grow. What we call "bad fortune" might offer more guidance than good. See how your circumstances are just what you need at the time they occur.

Now ask: "If this problem was designed for my benefit, what lesson would I gain?" Awareness will provide an answer. It will show you pain's purpose, and if awareness sees clear to the bottom it will show you a route to love.

Suppose pain stems from a child's special needs. What if the circumstance was designed for your benefit? In the light of awareness a handicapped child could be the perfect vehicle to acceptance. Acceptance allows the heart to open. This is prerequisite for love.

Consider a "bad marriage." Day-to-day it is nothing but misery, but the light of awareness shows lessons tailored just for you. You might see your partner's suffering. You might see self-interest as causing your own. You might find that self-interest measures your distance from love. Processed through awareness, "nothing but misery" becomes guidance to happiness.

What about a boss who makes your life miserable? If this circumstance was tailored for you, what would you gain? Could it point to some deeper life purpose? Could it be a way to bring you closer to loved-ones who care? Could it be both of these and more? See the predicament as for your benefit and the boss is holding a ladder for you.

What if pain stems from some failure to forgive, something you have done that you can not forgive yourself for, or from something done to you? Again awareness is the solution. Understanding and acceptance permit outflow of love.

Let pain call you to awareness and you see why pain must be and should be. Note however, that you cannot apply this to others. You cannot say: "Your suffering is good," or "I know what your pain means." As Ram Dass teaches, each person can access his own wisdom. Do so and you may find an escape hatch from suffering.

Awareness Exercise Two: What Would a Person of Wisdom Do?

A life circumstance may be the cause of dis-ease. It might pose a problem that makes for a "tough decision" where no answer is obvious. If this is the case, approach the problem after your daily practice session. Ask yourself this: "What would a wise person do?"

You may be surprised to find that there *is* an obvious answer.

Now ask yourself where this answer came from?

It came from you, a person of wisdom. That person becomes more and more present as awareness is restored. Wisdom becomes more accessible with continued practice.

Awareness Exercise Three: "Love Factory" Up and Running?

One day carpet shopping a plush wall-to-wall sample caught my eye. To my surprise it was made of one hundred percent recycled plastic bottles. Imagine that. Garbage processed in a factory was transformed into something beautiful and useful. You can do the same with life's garbage: pain.

With awareness, pain can be transformed into love. Awareness does the processing. First it breaks pain down into two things you may never have known were there: meaning and purpose. These let you see the usefulness of pain. Here meaningless suffering ends.

Apply this processing to the trials of having a child with special needs, to the misery of a "bad marriage," to problems with the boss, etc. Apply it to forgiving and you will see that pain can be transformed into love. To be sure your Love Factory is up and running check for the following:

- Check for "seeing yourself in it." Look closely. Is "seeing yourself in it" narrowing your view, blinding you to solutions to life's problems? At the source of your problem can you find a limited capacity for love? Remember: unhappiness is wanting something for yourself; pain feedback telling us we are going the wrong way.

Is it possible that what you call "love," what you actually *feel as love,* is not love at all, but love's opposite? Could it be self-gratification (as I experienced with the haircut)? Is it possible you could be mistaking taking for giving? Chapter Five's Love Tests may be useful here. To trade a stress manufacturing plant for a Love Factory, look for self-interest as the cause of pain.

- Check for awareness. A five-percent limit on awareness blinds us to guidance that is always present. You may be missing ninety five percent of guidance that should be yours. Look for low awareness at the root of dis-ease.

Love is an act of awareness; awareness an act of love. Has your love grown? Check for awareness. If awareness is present, your Love Factory is in operation.

- Check for a spiritual connection. Much of life's pain stems from "disconnection syndrome" as Dr. Weil calls it. Isolation prevents love's flow. A spiritual connection, as we will see later, is the ultimate love test.

"God is love" in Christian tradition. Think of your relationship to another human being as your connection to God. How good is your connection? Chapter Thirteen looks into the spiritual side of awareness. Now let's look at the power of awareness in prevention of dis-ease.

A Higher Standard: Awareness and Prevention

A Zen monk was asked to speak at the funeral of a public official. He did, but he returned to the monastery upset. He had been nervous while speaking and was determined never to let this happen again. The nervousness we call "normal" was not acceptable to the monk. He had a higher standard.

- A Higher Standard

Meditation makes a higher standard of mental health possible because it builds awareness. It restores contact with reality: sanity itself. That is why Hindu tradition calls meditation a "cure for mental illness." As the noisy tenant quiets, dis-ease we know as normal declines. (Chapter Two Self-tests reflect healing changes that occur as body is corrected and balanced.)

If we are continuously aware, dis-ease can be prevented. Understanding and acceptance guard us against it. In this way awareness lets us set a higher standard. It makes it possible to be saner than normal.

I found evidence of this when the SQ questionnaire was sent to long-term meditators living in retreat centers. I recall at least one perfect score. Studies of highly advanced meditators find them "apparently free of psychological conflicts usually considered an inescapable part of human existence (Walsh, 1993, page 36)."

This higher standard is reflected in the teachings of Karate dō. There we see higher expectation of human potential than we have yet realized. Let's review these teachings.

The Teachings of Karate dō

First, "life should be like looking in a pool of water clear and cool." This describes the calm of deep awareness. Awareness is like an oasis you can take with you. If you do, you stay clear and cool no matter what.

You should "see clear to the bottom." A higher standard is evident again here. It means, free of confusion and illusion, you see "what is" (reality). Seeing deeply you see why what is must be and should be.

This is the understanding awareness brings, understanding that leads to acceptance.

You should not "see yourself in it." This is the high aspiration to a life free of self-consciousness, self-absorption and self-interest, and fully consistent with reality. Selflessness affords union, full-functioning of your human nature, full capacity for love. Dis-ease ends when the "taker program" stops running. When you do not "see yourself in it," wanting something for yourself is no more.

Prevention enters with the next teaching: "you must not let anyone throw a pebble into your pool." A pebble would cause ripples and destroy your clarity. When someone insults you for instance, if you see no self in it, awareness guards your pool. Understanding its source you stay clear and cool.

More importantly, says Master Deac: "you must not throw a pebble in yourself." This is worse. In this enlightened philosophy you are considered responsible for your own thoughts. MoKow said: "Take nothing into tomorrow that will hinder you from moving forward." Here you are assumed to be Monarch of Mind. With this higher sanity you preserve your own clarity. When you are better than normal, victim and helplessness are no more.

Better than Normal

Awareness restores "the calm," as Master Deac calls it. Maintaining the calm requires continuous awareness. This means a constantly guarded pool, profound sanity, and prevention.

What we call "normalcy" is maintenance-level sanity. It is in the middle of a broad range of possibilities. Perfect sanity (full contact with reality; full awareness), is at one end. Insanity is at the opposite pole, delusions and hallucinations being gross departures from awareness. Insanity is not being "out of your mind," but being *in it*, totally lost in thought, as far from awareness as it is possible to be.

And so we see how meditation earned its title as a "cure for mental illness." Cultivating and maintaining awareness, mental health becomes something you can excel at, just as you can excel at physical conditioning. A few decades ago we thought the ideal pulse was seventy-six beats per minute. We thought normal was the best we could do. Now we know that with physical conditioning we can have the lower, better-than-normal pulse of an athlete. It may be that mental health warrants the same kind of revision. Normal is not the best we can do. We can aim higher. We can "acquire the calm." A "balance of mind never upset by any event under the canopy of heaven," gives us prevention.

- Aim for Prevention

As the Zen story goes, a girl living near a monastery became pregnant. Not wanting to incriminate her lover she named the monastery's renowned Abbott as the baby's father. Her parents confronted the monk with this. "Is that so?" answered the Abbott.

When the baby was born they went to the monk saying: "This is your baby." Accepting the infant the monk said: "Is that so?"

In time the girl wanted her baby back and revealed the identity of the father. They went and told the monk. "Is that so?" he said.

The Abbott had the calm. Seeing no self in it, his pool was perfectly guarded. He let no one throw a pebble into his pool. He threw none in himself. Immunity to suffering came from awareness with its understanding, acceptance and love. He required nothing to be other than it is. He had perfect mental balance. It is possible to stay this clear and cool, to "acquire the calm." What it takes is awareness.

"The Calm" in Martial Tradition

In martial arts training says Master Deac, "acquiring the calm" is learning not to be intimidated. Master Deac has the commanding presence of a fierce warrior. His body is rock hard, his power terrifying, yet he is capable of humility. He teaches through living example that we can survive, and not just survive but be victorious. He dives more courageously into life than anyone I know. How he and Master Choe met is an interesting story.

At age nineteen Master Deac was a Black Beret Army Ranger in the Korean conflict, a member of the famed 27th regimental combat team, the Wolf Hounds. At that time Master Choe age forty, was in army intelligence, acting as translator and teaching the troops hand-to-hand combat.

It was roll call. The troops lined up and the officer shouted their names. When he came to Cataldo he mispronounced it. "Calado," he shouted. No response came from the line. "Calatto...Catlado," he fumbled. Still no response from the line. Under his breath, the soldier next to Deac pleaded: "For God's sake answer him," but the young soldier waited for his name to be pronounced correctly.

When it was, he answered. The officer, hiding his anger, approached him. "Do you know my name and how to pronounce it?" he asked. Master Deac did and the officer moved on. That evening however, he summoned the soldier. He had set up an arena, a sort of boxing ring. He called the young soldier into the center and ordered him to hit him in the jaw.

Master Deac hesitated but the order was repeated and he complied. The response was severe. Deac was beaten to the ground. When he rose, the command was repeated. Again he was beaten to the ground. This continued until he was bloodied and barely able to stand.

Then a Chinese man, small in stature appeared and intervened. "That's enough," he said. "No," protested the officer. "I'm not through with him." Master Choe was now the intimidator. "Enough!" he ordered, and the officer backed down.

Master Choe helped Deac to Choe's quarters and tended his wounds. Then in broken English he asked for Deac's attention. He performed a simple, precision move in the air and demonstrated this a second and a third time. Master Deac said: "You do that very well." Thus a Master found his disciple.

When Master Deac describes Master Choe, you can almost feel Choe's calm. When he walked, even in combat boots, his torso and head were still and he seemed to glide. In a room full of people where others wasted energy in needless movement, turning and craning their necks, he moved only his eyes. Master Deac once saw him resting his head on a container of explosive gas. The concept "explosive gas" alarms people, but not someone in touch with reality enough to know that a sealed container is not dangerous. Deac was awed: "Where did this man come from? **Where did he come from?**"

Master Choe was steeped in calm, raised in a Buddhist monastery from age six to twenty as MoKow's disciple. Acquiring the calm he was free of confusion and illusion. His thinking mind, far from being a noisy trouble-making tenant, was his ally. A perfectly guarded pool put him beyond intimidation. He realized the high standard where victim and helplessness do not exist. His control however, was not dominance, not getting a grip on himself. In perfect control, no control is necessary.

Restore awareness, and your pool is guarded. With the noisy tenant subdued, toxic programs shut down. Right thought and action arise naturally from contact with reality. The chauffeur needs no compass. Contact with reality affords a big picture in which you see meaning and purpose, and through these you move in the direction of love.

Getting a Big Picture

"Enlarge," Deacsan, said Master Choe. *Enlarge.*

Awareness enlarges your picture, broadens your perspective. Victim and helplessness disappear, and meaning and purpose light your way.

All pain can be useful because you can *always* increase awareness. That means you can always grow in love.

I saw a news report of an elderly man whose wife was senselessly murdered by a troubled youth. Afterward he could not rest. He needed to understand how this tragedy could have happened. He found understanding and became a counselor and friend to troubled youth. Through awareness, even in this desperate circumstance, the love factory turned out a new life of purpose.

Enlarge your picture and you find purpose. See why what is should be and you know why you are living your particular life. If you are trapped at home struggling endlessly with fatigue, you might find this important work, more important for you right now than any possible occupation. When bad turns to worse you may see a higher calling, "God raising the bar" so to speak. Gravely ill you might see another, more important possibility of healing, an avenue to new life.

Awareness takes you from what pain is about (the problem) to what it is for (the solution awareness holds). Bigger pictures, like those that come from Awareness Exercise One, reveal life's meaning and purpose. Trust this exercise. It will work for you because in the Plan with the capital "P," no one is more important than you are.

Do not try to puzzle a big picture out. Vision expands when puzzles fade away. Words will be only noise here. Stay in what has been called a "concept-free zone." Concepts block your light and will bar still deeper understanding later. In time your view may enlarge enough to encompass your destiny.

A Tibetan prayer says: Grant I be given appropriate pain and suffering so that my heart may be truly awakened. When in pain remember you have a choice. Pain can be useful or it can be meaningless suffering. For pain to be useful, awareness is all you need.

CHAPTER EIGHT
TROUBLE-SHOOTING

Seven times knocked down; eight times get up.

Buddha

What you need to know: Success comes from effective practice. This Chapter helps you to be and to stay effective.

Every problem has a solution. You might find yours in the Trouble-Shooter's Checklist (page 106). If not, look below for help. These are the everyday problems covered here:

1. Resistance.
2. Distractions.
3. Wandering Thoughts.
4. Drowsiness.
5. Fidgety Practice.
6. Discomfort.
7. Boredom.
8. Emerging Too Soon.
9. Seeing No Progress.
10. Less Feedback.
11. No Feedback.
12. Anxiety.
13. Can't Stop Trying.
14. No Support At Home.
15. Skipping Sessions.
16. Having Doubts.
17. Low Motivation.

TROUBLE SHOOTER'S CHECKLIST

	Turn on the Juice	Get More Sleep	Another Position	Room too Warm?	Brisk Walk may Help	Stretch and Start Again	This Will Pass	Five Minute Limit	Avoid Short Sessions	Go to Beginner Practice	Try New Site	Eat After Practice	See Chapter 9	Rethink 'Prime Time'
Having Doubts?	☑						☑							
Distractions	☑						☑						☑	
Fidgety Practice	☑		☑			☑								☑
Discomfort			☑			☑					☑			
Bored with Practice	☑		☑	☑	☑						☑		☑	
Emerging Too Soon	☑		☑			☑			☑		☑	☑	☑	☑
Less Feedback	☑							☑			☑		☑	
Wandering Thoughts	☑							☑					☑	
Anxiety During Practice										☑				☑
No Feedback	☑							☑					☑	☑
Drowsiness	☑	☑	☑	☑	☑								☑	☑
Skipping Sessions			☑							☑	☑		☑	
Low Motivation	☑	☑								☑	☑		☑	

106

Problem 1: Resistance.

The noisy tenant does not want to be subdued and everyone feels resistance to practice at some point. It might be hard to break from your day, or you may be too restless to sit. These exercises can help you settle in. ("I" indicates imagery.)

- To Settle in, Be There.

Getting practice going is like rolling a boulder. It is hard at first but once the ball is rolling it gets easier. To help get yourself rolling, *be there.*

Become aware of the surface you are resting on. Sense the walls, the floor and the ceiling above. Take in colors, textures, a clock's tick, a fan's whir. Center yourself in your surroundings and you will *be there* ready to attend.

- To Settle in, Set a Mood. (I)

Setting a mood can end resistance. It can give you a frame of mind conducive to practice. Close your eyes and imagine how it might feel to be:

- A raft belonging to no one, adrift on still water.
- A point of light dead center in a bowling ball locked in a vault.
- A night owl awaiting dawn.
- A strand of seaweed rooted in the ocean's depth.
- Warm vapor rising through cool night air.
- A sun shining in a universe all its own.

Imagining these can put a noisy tenant in a favorable mood for practice. Try one now and another tomorrow.

- To Settle in, Put Everything Behind You. (I)

At practice time, do other things compete for attention? Put them all behind you.

Lie down, close your eyes and picture your work place. It might be an office piled with papers or a kitchen stacked with dishes. Imagine a zipper stretching top to bottom in this picture. Reach up and pull the zipper all the way to the floor. Then slip through to the other side, leaving it all behind you.

Now all you experience is deep velvet darkness. You are ready to begin.

- ## To Settle in, Lock On. (I)

Sit down to practice *deliberately*. Lock on to the disc like a laser beam extending from your eye to the bull's eye. When feedback appears, lock on to that.

- ## To Settle in, Imagine You Are the Teacher.

Imagine you are the teacher. What would you tell a student with resistance problems?

Awareness holds the answers. Tap the resources of a person of wisdom.

- ## To Settle in, Set a Five Minute Limit.

Set a five-minute limit. Take five minutes if you need to and let your mind run riot. Get what you are thinking out of your system. (Plan the day; write the shopping list or whatever.) Then remember what you are here for. Command "ATTENTION!"

Problem 2: Distractions.

Beginner practice goes like this. You settle in, a dog barks and you lose attention. You start again. Someone in the next room talks and you are back where you started. Distraction is inevitable, but note that the distraction is not what you hear. It is what you think. ("That darn dog;" "If only I had a quiet place," etc.) The noisy tenant, not the noise, is responsible for distraction.

Shelter beginner practice in a quite place. Later you will find that full awareness is beyond distraction. Advanced practice can be done in Grand Central Station.

Problem 3: Wandering Thoughts.

Throughout the centuries, meditation traditions echo the same concern:

Restless man's mind...
How shall he tame it?
Truly I think
The wind is no wilder.

How shall he tame it?

Tame it with *feedback*. Holding on to attention eliminates wandering. Be empowered by this. When your eyes meet the disc it is Contact! Dull and dreamy becomes sharp and clear. Tame it with feedback.

Problem 4: Drowsiness.

Drowsy practice is habit forming. Practice drowsy today and you will probably do so tomorrow.

If you are drowsy find out why. Is it too early or too late in the day? Are you sluggish from a recent meal? Are bad carbohydrates in your diet causing energy slumps? Is the room too warm? Are you slumped in a chair or on your toes?

Drowsiness is likely to be a motivation problem. See Chapter Nine (How to Stay Motivated, page 117). Strong motivation can prevent drowsiness and most other problems from arising.

Problem 5: Fidgety Practice.

Are you restless and fidgeting?

In advanced practice you can stop this by simply putting your foot down. Until then use the tips for settling in (page 107), or let off steam with exercise or stretches.

If fidgeting means: I'd rather be doing something else however, tend to motivation. When motivation is strong you will feel what Thoreau felt as he sat in solitude in the forest. "If the trees and flowers tried me by their standards," he wrote, "I would not have been found wanting." Imagine that feeling.

Problem 6: Pain and Discomfort.

Attention is your goal and pain disrupts attention. It also makes it less likely you will practice tomorrow. Pain problems must be addressed.

Check to see if pain stems from one of these:

-   The Wrong Sitting Position

Have you seen pictures of Chinese peasants in rice paddies? After bending for years they stand bent too. This is because posture habits become the body's structure over time. That is why our posture history rules out the cross-legged lotus position for most Westerners. If you are in pain it could be your sitting position.

- Poor Posture

Work toward a sitting posture that is erect *and* comfortable. Use pillows and props if necessary. If discomfort persists, try bodywork. Posture re-training (the Alexander Technique) or posture correction (Rolfing), might help.

- Unnecessary Tension

Straining to concentrate causes tension. In grade school when the teacher said: "Pay attention," we clenched teeth, made fists and wrinkled our foreheads. We were trying to show the teacher we were attending. We have confused tension and attention ever since.

Tension is *not* necessary for attention. Consider how a cat stalks a mouse. It sees the slightest movement, hears the faintest sound. It attends with its whole body yet its movements are supple and relaxed. Next practice session try this: stalk feedback the way a cat stalks a mouse.

Problem 7: Boredom.

Novelty creates interest. Thus for beginners, attention practice is an exciting adventure into the unknown. In advanced practice a new adventure begins and new excitement keeps you going. Between beginner and advanced levels however, be on guard for boredom. Do not let it slow you down. Use the alternate exercises (see Exercise Index, Appendix, page 217), and use the suggestions in Chapter Nine (page 117). Boredom is a problem you can solve.

Problem 8: Emerging Too Soon.

Emerging too soon is highly habit forming. Cut today's session short and you will probably do the same tomorrow. Never do less than fifteen minutes per session.

Problem 9: No Progress.

Are there stretches of time when you see no benefit?

You may be practicing at the wrong level. Verify your skill level with the Self-tests.

With efficient practice, every minute you invest pays off. Effects often kick in when least expected. Progress can take sudden leaps. You will not see it daily but you are making progress.

Problem 10: Less Feedback.

Practice sessions vary. Some days you will have more feedback, some less. There will be lively and dull, rich and poor practice. Quieting the mind can be like blowing out a candle or it can be like putting out a tire fire.

As practice skill increases, feedback comes more easily. Then it serves as a trusty watchdog, alerting you to daydreams and drowsiness, holding you on course. With feedback comes reliable benefit.

If you are getting less feedback than before, fix the problem. These tips will help you fight your way back and get on course again.

- *Draw a line.* Draw a clear line between doing this and not doing it.
- *Orient yourself.* Orient yourself before sitting. Know what you are about to do.
- *Improve your posture.* Think of yourself as a fighter taking on an opponent in the ring. Confront your noisy tenant with a good fighting stance: your best posture.
- *Address the disc.* Address the disc the way a golfer addresses the ball. Fix on the disc. Affirm: "I am attention."
- *Set a feedback quota.* Set a quota and aim for a little more feedback than you have been having, and most importantly,
- *Don't slack off.*

Problem 11: No Feedback.

If you are getting *no* feedback it means only one thing: you are *not* paying attention.

It is easy to kid ourselves saying we "put the time in." Amount of attention however, not amount of practice time is what counts. Ten minutes of practice with feedback is a powerhouse. Without feedback, sitting for hours may bring no benefit at all. You may be missing the mark by a wide margin and never even know it.

Remember: attention is a skill and feedback is necessary for skill learning. Take advantage of its precision guidance.

Problem 12: No Support At Home.

A meditation Master spoke before a large gathering: "If I were to tell you anything of what I really, deeply know, you would not believe me...If I were to give you any statement of the amazing reality behind what you imagine to be reality, you wouldn't credit it." Someone in the audience objected: "Surely you don't expect anyone to believe that!"

I think this shows why enlightened beings keep quiet. Centered in truth, words can sound like nonsense. Be prepared for misunderstandings. You will find them everywhere, including at home.

On vacation with my family in Maine I was perched on a cliff near our cottage, focusing on the shimmering water. Hours passed. Clouds gathered. It began to rain and I stayed. My awareness was so complete I was the rain itself. From the cabin I heard: "Is she out there in the rain?" "She's doing her thing," someone answered. "She has no idea it's raining." The misunderstanding could not have been greater.

Students tell amusing tales of misunderstandings. One woman told her family she needed time alone and undisturbed, and every evening she went to her room and closed the door. One night her teenage son forgot her request. He burst into her room and saw her sitting in dim light, gazing at the disc. "Oh mother," he said. "You'll never lose any weight that way."

A woman who practiced in her bedroom with the door closed, was home alone one day and decided for a change to use the living room. She positioned the disc and set to work. A few minutes later her Scottish terrier came in. He stopped several feet away and looked at the disc. Then he looked at her. Then he looked back at the disc, then back at her again. Apparently he could not figure it out either.

If there is a small child in your life, that child may understand this better than adults do. My little girl had a friend over one day. For twenty minutes they ran in circles screaming. I did not want to end the fun but a point came when I could no longer stand the noise. I told my daughter this and she said: "Just do your thing, Mommy. Then the noise won't bother you at all."

The very young intuit what this is. Adults however, confined to rigid, self-limiting concepts have no idea what is possible. Unfortunately, what you are doing here fits into most Westerners' "impossible" category. Until they experience this, nobody understands it. *Nobody.* Be prepared for: "What are you doing *that* for?" and, "Are you *still* doing that," and do it anyway.

Problem 13: Can't Stop Trying?

Bart Simpson was told: "Try to behave." His answer: "I can't promise I'll try, but I'll try to try." Something is wrong with trying.

Running down the driveway to catch her ride to nursery school, my daughter hollered back: "I like the drink you packed in my lunch Mommy." "I'll try to pack one for you every day," I answered. She stopped, turned and looked at me with compassion. "You don't have to *try*, Mommy," she said. "Just do it." The Master had spoken.

"Shall I try for it," asks the student?

"If you try you'll miss it," says the Master. "Penetrate the way of no-trying, it will be wide open—empty and vast (*Essential Zen*, 1994, page 21)."

"The way of no-trying" is the chauffeur's way of getting there. Without trying to change, change occurs. Without trying to be mindful you are mindful. Without trying to be filled, the emptiness is gone. Without seeking happiness, happiness comes free.

Wishing and hoping for success is natural, but when you sit down to practice, leave all that behind. Go the route that is wide open, empty and vast. As my little one said: "Just do it."

Problem 14: Anxiety.

Beginners are sometimes afraid of silence. As explained in Chapter Four, our concepts have created deep-rooted bias against it. We believe we are supposed to be thinking continuously. We see it as fundamental to existence. Silence seems unnatural.

Simply doing the exercise proves there is nothing in silence to fear. Soon we see another possibility: that we are supposed to be aware continuously; that awareness can be a fundamental mode of existence. Stay with the relaxing effortless "A" from Chapter Two if you like. Move on when it feels right. (When it feels right, it is right).

Problem 15: Skipping Sessions.

Attention focusing is simple and easy but you have to stay with it. If you are skipping sessions, check for poor excuses like these:
- Your energy is low. Skillful practice *builds* energy even when the energy you bring to it is low.
- You will make up the missed session later. Don't count on this.

- Spending time practicing seems selfish. To the extent this benefits you, your world will benefit.
- Too old to change. It is said that "the flint, lying under water for a hundred years, when taken out and struck, emits sparks." The same applies to coming to life through awareness.
- It is difficult to do. Think of it this way: what could be easier than gazing at a spot on the floor?
- Feel like your "old self" again? Remember who got you into trouble in the first place.
- Doing tapes instead? Tapes can not substitute here. Awareness builds like muscle. It takes an attention workout.
- An 'off' day? You can practice even on an 'off' day. Bring it the day's tone, down or up, bright or dull, tense or relaxed. Charge into it or ease into it but do it. Practice as if your life depends on it because it does. Do it, and do it *now*.

Do It Now

Do not wait until you feel you urgently need this. Practice *now*.

I once stood on a bridge looking down at a fast moving stream. A plastic bottle was trapped in the current, spun round and battered on rocks. Now and then however, it drifted into calm eddies near the bank and there for a while it was still. I saw that in those calm intervals it could easily be retrieved, but not otherwise.

The noisy tenant acts something like this. Sometimes the mind drifts. Sometimes it is trapped in forceful currents. At times it is easier to get free than at others. Without warning we can be engulfed in turbulence, family problems, financial troubles or illness. When you need most to be free, awareness can be hardest to come by.

As recommended in Chapter Seven, restore and maintain awareness and prevention is possible. That is why it is vital to practice now. Practice well, maintain "the calm," and when life gets turbulent, you will not get battered. If you are trapped in a current now and have discontinued practice, start again as soon as possible. "Seven times knocked down, eight times get up!"

Problem 16: Having Doubts?

Doubt can easily become "the greatest thing" and lead you off course. If you are having doubts, do not give in to them.

At a party I asked a man: "Do you meditate?" He said: "Well...not intentionally." Everyone laughed. I knew why the joke was so funny. How could "contemplating your navel" be of any benefit? I like to substitute "attention focusing" or "feedback exercise" for the word "meditation." The word "meditation" lacks positive connotations for many in the Western world.

If you have doubts however, they are not necessarily a drawback. Skepticism can work in your favor. Doubting is better than expecting miracles. Miracles do not require workouts and this does.

Doubts can actually be paths to certainty. They can move you to understand how and why this works. You might discover something surprising: that this works even if you think it will not. Just as skeptical joggers gain aerobic fitness, doubters progress here in spite of doubts. The best policy is to allow doubts to resolve simply by not giving in to them.

Problem 17: Low Motivation.

Of all the problems that interfere with practice, low motivation is the most serious you will face. It can keep you from practicing, and if you do practice it will make your practice less effective. Motivation calls for a separate chapter. This comes next.

CHAPTER NINE
HOW TO STAY MOTIVATED

The one thing indispensable is to persevere.
Hubert Benoit

What you need to know: Motivation is all-important. Do not leave it to chance. This chapter can help you stay motivated and it can make good motivation even better.

One fine summer day my little girl surprised me by taking a schoolbook outside to read. Minutes later she came back in. "I can't read," she said. "The butterflies are bothering me."

There is a lesson here. Her problem was not really the butterflies. It was her low motivation to read. Most problems that interfere with practice are like those butterflies. "Too little time" and "too much to do" do not stop you. Low motivation does. With enough motivation, nothing can stop you.

This chapter shows fifteen ways to help build a strong practice habit. First and foremost, set a time and stick to it.

1.   Set a Time and Stick to It.
We do not look for excuses not to brush our teeth. At set times we just do it. Establish a daily practice routine. Set a time, stick to it and practice will become as automatic as brushing your teeth.

2.   Badger Yourself.
Most things we need to do call out to be done. The car's gas gauge registers low; the disordered house looks a mess and we act on these things. Disordered minds however feel normal to us. That is why you need to remind yourself to practice. Put it in your palm pilot; mark it on your calendar; leave notes on your mirror. Badger yourself until practice becomes automatic.

3.   Take a Bribe.

Pair the exercise with some small reward you give yourself for sitting down. Would a cup of tea or cocoa entice you to break from your day? Do not hesitate to bribe yourself if necessary.

4.   Remember that Pork Chop.

A woman I taught suffered from social anxiety and a fear of choking. She was limited to soft food. After a few months of practice she found herself sitting in a crowded restaurant enjoying a pork chop. Afterward the memory of that brought her back to practice again and again.

What have you experienced that proves the power of your practice? Remember it. Like the memory of that pork chop, it will bring you back.

5.   Make Time.

Short on time? Consider a time management suggestion. Suppose you have three large stones and many small ones and you want to fit them in a jar. Put the small stones in first and the large will not fit, but when the large go in first, the little ones fit easily around them. The lesson is *first things first.* Give your practice priority and the rest of your life will fit around it.

Another suggestion is to do two things at once. Practice while dinner cooks or the clothes wash. Take a bus to work and do it on the way. If you do not have time you can make time.

6.   Get Psyched.

Suppose you were a gymnast about to perform. Imagine the effect on performance of not wanting to. You can expect the same from not wanting to practice.

Now imagine the effect of being eager to perform and certain you will win. Expect the same from wanting to practice. **Motivational books and tapes can help you get psyched.** You might try *One Hundred Ways to Motivate Yourself* (Steve Chandler, 2004), or *Enthusiasm Makes the Difference* (Norman Vincent Peale, 1967).

7.   Don't Look for Results.

Do not expect to see change every day. Progress here is like applying fine coats of varnish to a piece of wood. You will not see a difference between today's and tomorrow's coat. Change occurs by imperceptible degrees, but one day what you see will take your breath away.

8.   Don't Take "No" for an Answer.

When you want to skip a session remember: the harder it is to sit down and practice *the more you need to*. Do not let butterflies bother you. Don't take "no" for an answer.

9.   Keep Records.

After much training with his Master, Deac remained frustrated by a difficult move. "I'll never get there," he said. Master Choe offered a suggestion. He said Deac's journey was like scaling a mountain, and he was now looking up at the peak and thinking how hard the climb. "Look back," he said. "See how far you have come and you will know the rest will be easy." Adopt this perspective and the hard climb becomes an ascent.

Go back and let the Self-tests show you your progress, and keep a record of practice time. This will let you see how far you have come.

10.   Use Pain.

A man with worsening lung disease could walk only a few steps. He found purpose in his pain through awareness created in meditation. All his life he had never stopped to experience the present. His illness forced him to, and for the first time he saw the beauty around him.

As we saw before, pain signals a need to restore awareness. Answer the call and pain becomes useful. You are not a victim if you let pain guide you. Let it move you to practice.

11.   Do it Until you *Want To*.

A man's practice freed him from painful ulcer symptoms, but the prospect of continuing to practice upset him. "Do I have to do this for the rest of my life," he asked?

I answered: "No. You *have to* do it only for a while. After that, you'll *want to*."

When pain ends, another form of motivation to practice takes over. When we begin, our aim is to escape anxiety, avoid stress, decrease tension, etc. We are running away from trouble.

Later however, we find ourselves moving toward a goal. Emptiness moves us at first. Awareness fills the emptiness. Then the gratification of fullness entices us on. Trade desperation for inspiration. Do it until you *want to.*

12. Don't Let Boredom Stop You.

There is no reason to let boredom stop you. Keep your practice fresh and interesting with these suggestions:

- *Change Something.* Any change can create interest. Try a new place; another time of day or an alternate feedback exercise (see Exercise Index, Appendix, page 217).
- *Apply Fertilizer.* Thinking can play a useful role in the transition to awareness. Use it as "fertilizer," as Master Deac teaches. Today's books and classics from the traditions can be powerful fertilizer. Do not spend *practice time* reading however. This is like swimming. You are nowhere until you dive in.
- *Have a Tea Ceremony.* Centuries ago, monks invigorated themselves before meditating in a ritual of awareness known as the Tea Ceremony. *The Book Of Tea* (Okakura, 1964) tells the story. You might have a tea ceremony of your own.
- *Do it for Someone Else.* A need to help yourself probably led you here. Now try doing your practice for someone else, or dedicate practice to some good purpose.
- *Invent your own Exercise.* Attention to anything restores awareness. Invent your own exercise. Attend with your ears for instance, instead of your eyes. Listen to snow fall.

Master Deac teaches this excellent exercise. Focus attention on a candle flame in a dark room. Then close your eyes and attend to the visual after-image. When it fades, focus again on the candle flame and repeat this sequence.

Use traditional meditation techniques if you like, but keep the disc handy. Confirmation of attention is what you need. Be sure you stay on target.

13. Link it to something you Love

Do you play tennis or golf? Are you in the performing arts? Do you have some form of creative expression like writing? If so, your practice will give you an edge. Here are some of the things you can gain.

The Awareness Edge in Sports

A philosopher wrote: "The mania of thinking renders us unfit for every activity." Awareness benefits *every* activity you perform. In sports and in the arts you become "a natural" as awareness sets performance free. Let's look first at sports.

Someone asked a professional golfer: "What goes on in your mind when you have to sink a putt for a huge sum of money?" He answered: "Nothing. If you're thinking you're in trouble."

In karate, a student with a wandering mind would break his hand, not the brick.

When hitting well, baseball star Ted Williams said he could see the seams on the pitched ball.

These are instances of an awareness edge. Tennis pro Timothy Gallwey had it. In *The Inner Game of Tennis* (1974) he taught the benefits of "the master skill—concentration: the act of focusing attention." "Blotting out thinking processes" brought him success on the court. "Self-consciousness," he said, "was not there to foul things up." His skill grew. He played spontaneously, focused on the ball, watched it, heard it, all senses participated. No thinking meant no indecision, no confusion. He had increased accuracy and power and an exhilarating sense of relaxation. Attention benefited his life too, so much in fact that where he first used concentration to improve his tennis, later he used tennis to increase concentration.

"Armed all the time:" Awareness in Karate

What Gallway discovered through tennis has long been known in Karate. In the West, martial arts are largely disconnected from philosophical-spiritual roots. At one time however, a monk's ability to meditate was believed to determine his fighting skill. Master Choe taught: "You must be armed all the time." He meant be aware. The advantages are endless. In Karate dō as in life "it is all awareness."

When you stop spilling yourself away, vital energy builds. In the East, this energy is called *chi* or *ki*. Master Deac has achieved "the uninterrupted flow of natural energy." Seeing his frictionless movement I feel the power of deep water moving. His vital energy is concentrated enough that its trace can be seen in his footprints after meditation. He has the perfect control of no control. Awareness does everything.

He once demonstrated his power with a clap on my shoulder blade. With little sensation of impact a seismic wave passed through me. It felt like I had jumped off a house. This power is not muscle strength. It is control of the flow of vital force through disciplined attention.

Awareness in Karate means keen senses, accuracy and ability to sense the opponent's intention. Awareness does not err like judgment. Because you are not "thinking-up" moves, no projection of intention gives you away. An opponent is taken by surprise.

When you are aware, no trying jams the machinery. Imagine a pianist "trying" to do a trill. Here two fingers alternate, striking keys faster than nerves conduct impulses from the brain to the fingers. "Trying" would make impossible what awareness does effortlessly.

"Judge quickly but not verbally," said Master Choe. Awareness is not slow and indecisive like thinking. You do not live through an interpreter. Bruce Lee described the perfect mental state as: "not thinking but not dreaming." Here, he said: "the hand strikes by itself." Awareness has no intention to act; no thought of action; no effort expended to achieve anything. "Mind and technique become one," and the deep relaxation this produces staves off fatigue.

What about fear? The noisy tenant pushes the panic button. With no judgment that something is fearful however, there is no fear. When your pool is guarded your face wears no expression. Master Deac says the opponent sees only your resolve. Looking into fearless eyes of resolve could be intimidating enough to end conflict before it begins.

In injury, awareness handles the problem of physical pain. The sensation is felt but not judged as "painful," and not judged as "my pain." It is felt without unnerving you.

Karate's aim of "purity and perfection" is elimination of self in trade for awareness. Once, doing my *kata* I was imagining myself fighting. I **was corrected** for doing "fantasy moves." I **was told**: "aim only to be present." Only be aware. Awareness is presence. Get your self out of the *kata* and your body moves as Master Deac's, and Master Choe's, and so on back through centuries of "magnificent men" (as Choe called them), aiming for perfection.

Master Deac says of perfection: "I strive for it." Master Choe however, taught him not to impose images of perfection on students to live up to. With disciplined attention, martial arts can evolve into enlightenment. If Karate is your sport, let this motivate your attention focusing practice.

Now see what awareness means for creativity.

Awareness and Creativity

A *bo* staff is a six foot long wooden pole used as a fighting tool. When Master Choe and his disciple were in Korea, the local *bo* champion came to challenge any takers. Master Choe accepted, saying his student "would win in one blow."

Deac was alarmed. He had never even held a *bo* staff. Master Choe however, had the awareness it takes to think outside the box. He knew *bo* fights began with a standard strike. He invented a strike to counter it. Master Deac used this, broke his opponent's *bo* and helmet, and won the fight in one blow.

Concepts box us in. Being creative without awareness is like trying to dance in a straight jacket. You can not be original while running programs.

Take creative writing. Concepts hold us in rigid patterns, mental ruts. Awareness cuts new paths through consciousness. Pulitzer Prize winner Alice Walker said she "needs space that is really clear for whatever is emerging to come." Picture a bubble at the bottom of a bowl of Jello. The bubble is an insight. With solid concepts in place it can not arise. When concepts become fluid and dissolve away, the barrier is gone and insight arises. Eckhart Tolle says: "If you have a spacious relationship with your thought processes, you no longer believe everything you think. Thoughts are just tiny fragments of many possibilities (from *Realizing the Power of Now*, 2007)." Full awareness is spacious enough for deepest truth to rise to the surface.

While writing this book, insight never came to me while sitting with my laptop. It came when I was not thinking, and the further from thinking I was, the deeper was the insight that arose. Degas said: "Only when he no longer knows what he is doing does the painter do good things." Work is not creative when we are thinking what everyone else is thinking. The great conductor Toscanini defined tradition as "the last bad performance." Even the piece most often played he performed as if for the first time. He told his musicians: "Forget the notes! Abandon yourself to the music." Abandon your self and nothing blocks awareness.

Awareness and Presence

The less self-absorbed you are the more absorbed you are in what you are doing. Put another way: the more aware you are, the more *there you are*. Awareness is presence, and in the performing arts the stronger your presence, the more you take the audience with you.

Prima ballerina Margot Fonteyn's magic was her presence. She told of meeting the famous actress Katherine Hepburn. "I'm so excited to meet *you*," said the actress. The ballerina was speechless. She had never seen herself as important. It was always "just the dance."

When aware, you are what you are doing. Master Deac says: "Be your target." Being what you are doing frees creative expression. Awareness brings forth "spontaneous forms from nowhere:"

> *Ch'ui the draftsman could draw more perfect circles freehand than with a compass. His fingers brought forth spontaneous forms from nowhere. His mind was free and without concern…no application was needed. His mind was perfectly simple and knew no obstacle* (Chuang Tzu, in Merton, 1965, page 112).

Again here, perfect control means no control is necessary. Awareness does it all.

14. Expect Surprises

"If we did the things we are capable of doing, we would literally astound ourselves," wrote Thomas Edison. Keep going and you may be astounded. You may be surprised by what Christian tradition calls:

> *Strength in weakness; silence in tumult; order in chaos; certainty in doubt; calm in crisis; light in darkness, forgetfulness in injuries, courage in alarms, resistance in temptation, peace in war, and quiet in tribulation* (Father Molinos, 1685).

All these benefits have something in common. They come as surprises. You will not know what you have gained until crisis arises or darkness descends. Power builds without your knowing it. Keep going and expect surprises.

Awareness may bring "psychic powers." South Pacific Island natives navigated to distant islands long before there were charts or navigational tools. They did not need them. They simply knew where the islands were. Such intuitive power comes from depths of awareness we have yet to fathom.

A few times in deep awareness, I have had an ability to forecast weather. I discovered this when I heard a forecast and somehow knew it was incorrect. I tried to understand how I knew, assuming my knowledge was based on subtle clues I had picked up. When I looked for them however, my power to know what the weather would be vanished, drowned in the noise of thinking.

My students have also reported surprises. One went for surgery expecting anxiety. She told me her husband, "the calm one" was nervous and she, "the nervous one," was calm. An anxious speaker found himself comfortable before an audience. A woman with a fear of snakes surprised herself by admiring the beauty of the skin of a snake she came upon suddenly in her yard.

Self-healing is another power that may be cultivated by attention practice. How we can "give life back to life" is an unexplored mystery. You can however expect surprises like finding aspirin in your cabinet long past its expiration date and realizing you have not had your usual headache perhaps for years. Someone might mention "a bad dream" and you will realize that these are no longer part of your life. When threatened you may find yourself filled with love and therefore fearless.

Later chapters will reveal more surprising powers of awareness. I think these will motivate and inspire you to practice by showing you how large you are.

Thoreau told of a strong and beautiful bug that came out of an old table that had stood in a farmer's kitchen for sixty years. It was heard gnawing its way out for several weeks, growing from an egg deposited in a living tree long before. We are encrusted like this, boxed in rigid concepts, buried in layers of opinion and judgment in a dead dry life of words. "Set free," wrote Thoreau, "who knows what beautiful and winged life may come forth to enjoy its perfect summer life at last!"

15. Improve your Practice

Improve your practice and inspiration will replace desperation. When this happens, motivation will take care of itself. Here are some ways to help advance your practice. First, try a retreat.

- To Advance, Retreat

To advance, retreat. *Sanctuaries* (Kelly, 1996) lists retreat houses and programs across the country.

A retreat may offer the inspiration of a teacher. A good teacher illustrates by example that more is possible. Master Deac inspires in this way. He is a warrior, the image of masculine authority. His physique is so developed he jokes about being bulletproof, yet he holds a baby as tenderly its mother does. He says in every man is a woman: in every woman, a man. He volunteers at a Veterans Hospital's End of Life unit, feeding people, bringing hope and laughter. Balance lets him function on all cylinders.

When Master Choe taught Deac how to use a sword, he took him to a thicket of pin willows. There Deac learned to wield the blade and slice through trunks with ease. Leaving the grove, Master Choe saw a flower his disciple had trampled on entering. He stood the flower up with his blade. "Too much warrior, Deac-san," he said, "not enough lover." Then gesturing to the blade he said: "It can do that too." Choe showed him that more is possible.

Master Deac's life proves the possibility of triumph over pain. The bloodiest war in history left him with nightmares and chronic pain from nerve damage from frostbite. Early trials included a young brother's death, and both alcohol and drug addiction. He was forged in a furnace and he emerged with a great human heart and lessons to share: we need not be victims; we can survive and we can be victorious. Still Master Deac reminds students: "I'm not going to walk you home." Dependence on a teacher bars independence.

- Don't be Dependant

Dependence on a teacher can be an obstacle to your development. A Zen nun wrote:

There is nothing you can do but to go your own way in life, walking on your own two feet...There is nothing but to stand erect, resisting any temptation to depend on others (Aoyama, 1990, page 40).

The words may seem extreme but they do apply to your growth through attention practice. This is a path of action not words. Just as a personal trainer can not build your muscles, a contact with reality workout can be done by you alone. Awareness can not be restored by teachings. Siddhartha said: "Teachings are of no use to me, they have nothing but words (in Hesse, 1995, page 142)." We mistake words for truth. Freedom from ignorance is actually freedom from what you now think you know. This includes *your teacher's concepts*.

Truth can be known only through awareness so on retreat, what counts is the silence in you, not in the retreat center. This job can be done by you alone. Every practice session is a solo flight. Basking in a teacher's bliss is a momentary joy. Go home with bliss of your own.

- Aim Higher.

To do it better, aim higher. Do not be intimidated by the words Great Liberation, Great Knowledge, Great Tranquility, and Great Love. Reaching these goals is a simple matter of seeing what is before your eyes. Feedback proves that you can do it.

Finally, remember the lesson of the butterflies. Watch out for problems of motivation in disguise. Watch out especially for: "I have something more important to do." There is no such thing! "You must go on," said Brother Lawrence, "making up your mind to persevere in it until death, whatever the difficulties may be."

CHAPTER TEN
ADVANCED PRACTICE

If you desire the great tranquility, prepare to sweat white beads.

Hakuin

If you feel at home with Chapter Six Self-tests it is time to board the rapid rail.

Here you will focus on the disc as before but you will have a new attitude. Until now you "let it happen." Now you can "make it happen." How? With *single-minded purpose.*

- Single-minded Purpose

What is single-minded purpose?

Suppose a car slips off a jack, pinning your child. You lift the car and hold it while the child inches out. What are the odds that you will forget what you are doing and let the car slip? It would be impossible because you have single-minded purpose. At that moment nothing else exists.

With single-minded purpose you can take charge. Attention is honed to razor-sharpness. With this you can "pass through the silver mountain and the iron wall."

A Zen Master said: "With teeth clenched and tongue pressed against the gums...by means of sheer mental effort hold back, crush and burn out the thought." Advanced practice feels like this, energetic and vigorous, the most active functioning of your day. You might even perspire as if exercising, but perspiration is not necessary, and neither are clenched teeth, just single-minded purpose. And what exactly is your purpose? What is your aim? It is *continuous* feedback.

- Aim for Continuous Feedback

Your aim is continuous feedback. Build up to it the way you would build up to running long distance. You need to run one mile before two, and four brings five in reach. Attention builds this way: short stretches of feedback make long ones possible. A stopwatch can help lengthen stretches.

Use a Stopwatch

Time your feedback with a stopwatch. The stopwatch function on a watch will do, but a hand-held stopwatch is better. Hold it loosely, thumb over the start button. Start timing when feedback begins. Stop when it stops. This way you will be answerable for every second.

These practice tips can also help lengthen stretches.

Advanced Practice Tips

• Set a Goal. Set a goal for your session, a feedback quota. Raise it as concentration builds.

• Don't *Try*, Just Do It. At work we rarely just work. We *try* to earn money, try to get ahead. Cleaning house, we do not just clean. We try to do it right; try to finish in a hurry. This trying divides attention, wastes energy and hinders performance. When you sit down to practice, do not try to get enlightened. Just do it.

• Sit Better. Beginners sit like puddles; advanced students like sculptures of pure energy. Practice improves when posture improves. Here is a way to sit better.

Put a barricade (a box or book) between you and the disc. Position it so the disc can not be seen until you straighten up. When better posture becomes a habit, reposition the barricade for still more erect posture.

Think of your posture as a fighting stance. It should be strong but poised, like a *tai chi* Master in a pose. Poise is suspension of activity in a condition of balance, as the earth is poised in space. Do not be a settled mass. Be poised like an object in space. Hold your body the way you want to hold your mind.

• Build On Your Success. To advance, build on your success.

If you started a business and the first quarter turned a profit, you might want to spend the earnings, relax or take a vacation. In advanced practice it is tempting to do the same: to ease up and glide on your success. Resist the temptation however, and success becomes a springboard. Put profits back into the business and you will deploy more power tomorrow.

- <u>Be Confident</u>. Feedback is proof of attention, and attention restores awareness. Be confident. You can not fail.

Now for some dos and don'ts.

Dos and Don'ts

- <u>Do Sit Right</u>. Sit to make it happen.

- <u>Do Hold Direction</u>. Don't hover around. Hold direction. Hold on to feedback and keep going straight.

- <u>Don't Relax</u>. Don't do a relaxation exercise. Do a contact-with-reality workout.

Extra Help: Attention Building Exercises

These exercises can increase your power of concentration.

Red Alert (I)

Imagine the disc is a radar screen and any change (distortion) on the screen is an enemy torpedo. The only way to stop it is to detect it and keep it in sight. Fix on feedback with RED ALERT vigilance.

Power Surge (I)

Have you ever misplaced your keys and needed them in a hurry? Remember the energy surge that went into the search? Bring the same to your practice.

Imagine a rheostat centered in your belly. Turn it up and feel the power surge when you turn on the juice. "Prepare to sweat white beads."

Waves of Attention (I)

This is a great way to start a session and well worth the time it takes to learn to use it.

Sit erect. Close your eyes and imagine sitting on the beach watching the surf. Wave after wave rolls gently in. Inhale slowly and deeply as each wave moves in. Exhale as it subsides.

When this pattern is established, make each wave a wave of attention. As it rolls in, increase your intensity of concentration. After it crests, release, relax and begin again. Build intensity with rising tide, wave after wave.

Now let these images fade and simply be waves of attention, building with each inhalation. Let your whole body participate.

Imagine that you are the Master (I)

Imagine that you are the Master. A large audience looks to you for help. Show them how it is done.

Advanced Self-Tests

At this practice level most questions can be answered through use of your own awareness. You need Self-tests however to guide you through this new terrain. Ninety-one are provided here measuring attention, awareness, and efficiency of practice technique.

Think of each test as a separate peak in a mountain range. These peaks are high; some extremely high. Do not expect to scale them all at once.

As before, asterisks indicate alternate feedback exercises for use in place of the disc (see Exercise Index, Appendix, page 217).

Self-test 84: Compulsive Reading?

Open a book to any page. Find an "o" and focus on it. Can you attend to "o" without reading words around it?

If you can not help reading words, can you at least keep from being carried away by their meaning?

Compulsive reading means an out-of-control tenant. Turn the page and try again.

Self-test 85: Effortless Practice?

Lifting weights is hard at first but the more you do it the easier it gets. The same goes for building your power of concentration.

Has attention come easy for you? Has your practice felt like smooth sailing with the wind at your back? Has it seemed like "it doing you," instead of you doing it?

Advanced practice can reach a point past all resistance where strain and strainer disappear and the chauffeur conveys you straight through. Such practice is a laser that cuts through steel.

Self-test 86: Are you Seeing a Glow?

Find one of your old baby pictures. Note the glow in your eyes when you smiled. Now look in the mirror. Can you see the same glow in your smile today?

Wayne Dyer illustrates the point with a picture of his grandson's smile. He writes: "there's an invisible force coming through what we see in the photo, and that's what we want to return to. If we could see our spiritual source with our eyes, we'd witness pure joy, ecstasy, happiness and peace (*Inspiration*, 2006, page 214)."

Returning to the source is the goal of practice. Can you see it glow in your eyes in your mirror?

You have big shoes to fill. They are your very own baby slippers.

Self-test 87: Five in Five?—A Test of Motivation.

Check your motivation. When you sit down to practice, how many minutes does it take you to get five minutes of feedback?

Like everyone, I have been kept from practice by other things. I remember a day of longing to practice while working, having guests, cleaning up after dinner, putting baby to bed. Finally free I walked to where I would sit and even before sitting, concentration was intense. That night I had five minutes of feedback in five practice minutes.

Five minutes of attention can take five minutes or it can take all day. Five in five proves powerful motivation. How long does it take you to get five minutes of feedback?

Self-test 88: Experience Gap?

An advanced student was asked why he was excited about his practice. He thought it over and said: "Well...the other day I saw a pebble and *Wow!*"

Two people shoulder-to-shoulder, one aware the other not, two different worlds. One sees a mind-made world. The other sees the miracle. One has a potted plant existence. The other: "Great Liberation." Searching for words to cross the divide feels like stepping off the end of the earth.

Like the student with the pebble, it is good if you can not explain your experience. The wider your experience gap the deeper your awareness. (That is why the knowing ones are silent.)

Self-test 89: Beyond Distraction?

The best practice is beyond distraction:

Sitting alone in great silence
Even though the heavens turn and the earth is upset,
You will not even wink (Nyogen Senzaki).

This is how perfect concentration feels. Have you felt it?

Self-test 90: Can you say: "Is that so?"

The Zen Master had perfect acceptance when he said "Is that so?" Test your acceptance. If someone said something offensive and untrue about you, could you say: "Is that so?"

Dis-ease is your distance from acceptance; your distance from awareness.

Self-test 91: A Body Check.

Dr. Weil sees "disconnection syndrome" as the cause of much illness. When awareness re-connects us and outflow of love occurs, the body returns to harmonious balance. Research indicates that "giving" benefits asthma and insomnia and improves recovery after heart attacks. Seniors who give have been found to live longer and there is evidence that altruism boosts the immune system (*Connections*, January, 1999, #5, Institute of Noetic Sciences, page 26). Correct and balance yourself and body is corrected and balanced too.

Review your "stop signs" from Chapter Seven (page 94). Is the list shorter? When you turn around your body turns around too.

Self-test 92: Getting Pain's Message?

The last time you had pain, how long did it take to find meaning and purpose in it?

A major problem in your life is like the seed of a great tree. Contained in it is everything needed to bring tree-hood to perfection. Gain its full lesson and you will realize perfection. There is no flaw in the grand scheme.

Self-test 93: The Ice Cube Test *

Put an ice cube in a dish and watch it melt. Your experience will tell you how advanced your practice is.

Beginners watch impatiently, eyes flitting, minds wandering. They miss the melting altogether. They see only that it has melted (a puddle suddenly appears). No beauty is experienced. No awe. No wonder.

Advanced students by contrast see diamonds liquefy before their eyes. The experience is unforgettable and pouring out the water afterward is a significant parting.

What do you see?

Self-test 94: Open to Beauty?

Look around. In deep awareness, ordinary sights are like great still life paintings. Do you see beauty?

Exceptional beauty can take us out of our everyday minds and into awareness. When aware to begin with however, you are continuously open to beauty. You do not need poets to point it out or artists to paint you a picture.

Great art is great because it brings you in contact with the reality the artist's awareness saw. Can you see through artists' eyes? Is there beauty in the pencil on your desk?

Not seeing beauty does not mean it is not there.

Self-test 95: Good or Bad?

The SQ Test in Chapter Two was pre-tested on college students. Item 1 at that time was "I talk to myself silently, continuously through the day." One woman looked at this, came up to me and asked: "Is this good, or bad?"

How would you have answered?

At the advanced practice level you should have an answer. You should now know what is meant by the Chinese saying: "Thought is the disease of the Western mind."

Self-test 96: Noise Tolerance?

When you began, it may have been hard to tolerate silence. Now it may be hard to tolerate noise.

Does TV or radio seem to offer you less than it once did?

This suggests clarity. When you have good reception you notice interference. Canned TV can not compete with the live show playing all around you all the time. You will not want noise anymore.

Self-test 97: True Experience? (I)

While practicing today, see if you can imagine your body as empty space like a holographic image?

If you can imagine this go further. Can you imagine no body at all, no you there, just the disc?

Is this not true experience?

Self-test 98: A Clean Break?

Recite in imagination "Mary had a little lamb," but stop short before "lamb."

For beginners "lamb" comes loud and clear, like it or not. Later you can stop a thought mid-sentence. At the highest practice level you can stop a word mid-syllable. When you can say: "Mary had a little lamb," without the "lamb," your tenant is thoroughly subdued.

Try again. "Mary had a little—."

"He that ruleth his spirit is better than he that taketh a city." Proverbs 16:32.

Self-test 99: Rate Attention.

Working with the disc, how much of you is focused? How much body? How much mind?

Rate attention on a scale from one to ten where one drifts and dreams and ten shakes the earth. Aim for perfect concentration. Turn your incubator on high.

Self-test 100: Deeper Understanding?

Shallow ponds are murky. The deeper the pond is the clearer the water. The same goes for awareness. As it deepens, you see deeper. Full awareness sees "clear to the bottom."

Review Self-tests from Chapter Six (page 77). Is your understanding deeper; broader; clearer? Test it on this: "One who hoards wealth while others are starving may kill more people than the cruelest murderer."

Deep awareness resonates the truth here. It sees through the "taker program" we run blindly with its self-centered values, wants and needs. Hoarding wealth is inconsistent with the reality of our true nature. Images of starvation are present to all of us at some deep level. "Having it all" prevents others from having any. Broad awareness understands this.

Self-test 101: Are you Still Waiting?

Are you waiting for something, the weekend, a vacation, retirement or maybe just waiting for a bus?

Waiting signifies emptiness. In full awareness full presence makes life complete continuously.

Are you still waiting?

Self-test 102: Kipling's Tests.

The poet Kipling offered some advice:

If you can dream and not make dreams your master,
If you can think, and not make thought your aim,
Yours is the earth and everything that's in it…

Break this down into three separate challenges. The first two tell if your tenant has taken over. The third measures the size of your mansion.

How do you score on Kipling's tests?

Self-test 103: Is Enough, Enough?

Do you have enough time? Enough money? Enough room? Enough stuff? Enough of *anything*?

With low awareness, enough is never enough. Emptiness can not be filled by adding more of anything except awareness. It is filled only by union. Awareness is "all-sufficing" so enough is always enough.

Self-test 104: Putting Yourself into It?

Position the disc and try hard to concentrate. For five minutes, put yourself into it.

Now do something different. Keep the intensity but do not put yourself into it. Can you feel a difference?

At first attention is willful. Later your practice carries you. If this still seems mysterious, think of your task as awareness instead of attention. Be intensely aware.

Self-test 105: Are you Fearless?

Are you fearless?

If you are grounded in truth, knowing that things are as they must be and should be, you can be free of fear. Such fearlessness however, comes with no feeling of courage or bravery. "One who is truly prepared does not appear to be prepared at all."

Are you fearless? If so, you are aware.

Self-test 106: A Priorities Test.

If you had only a certain amount of time left to live would your priorities change? Would you want joy, clarity and peace more than what you are pursuing now?

Well you *do* have only a certain amount of time left to live. Test your priorities.

In monasteries when the chapel bell rings, monks stop what they are doing and return to their spiritual center. Pick a day and set an alarm to go off randomly several times. See if you can drop what you are doing and return to your center. If you can your priorities are well in place.

Self-test 107: Can you Land like an Ant?

My little girl watched as someone skimmed a frog from the pool and hurled it away. "Will it hurt the frog," she asked? "No," said the quick thinker, "he lands like an ant."

If someone insults you, can you "land like an ant?" If no ego needs defending, there is nothing heavy there to crash and insults are not insulting. You can be clear enough not to take offense.

If someone offends you, make it a Self-test.

Self-test 108: What is Wrong with this Picture?

Consider the Hindu view of human nature: "Arise, O resplendent Being, thou who art forever pure, thou who know'st neither birth, nor death, arise, All-Powerful, and manifest thy nature."

One word here is misleading. Which is it?

"Forever" is not the problem word. Original perfection is beyond corruption. The problem word is "Arise."

If you had a fine oak floor covered by old carpeting, commanding it to arise would serve no purpose. You would get to work removing what conceals it. The same goes for your true nature. All that is said of the forever pure is true, but beckoning it forth is whistling in the wind.

Self-test 109: Can You Guess?

The sage Lao Tzu wrote:

The King of life goes his way free,
Keeps his roots down in the origin,
Down in the spring,
And opens a great heart...a world's refuge.

Can you guess what he meant by "the origin; the spring?"

(As Master Deac says: "It is all awareness, awareness, awareness.")

Self-test 110: How Word-bound are You?

When someone speaks, is your understanding limited to the meaning of the words?

Words keep you at the level of thinking, and thinking is very far from knowing. The first time I met Master Deac he said: "How can you teach if you can be intimidated?" I had not told him I wanted to teach or how intimidated I was by the prospect.

Awareness is knowing. At this practice level you will sometimes disregard words and see their source instead. You will be less word-bound over time.

Self-test 111: The Smile Test. (I)

Pause a moment and imagine passing someone on the street. Return their smile.

Did your smile start with your mouth?

If a smile starts with your mouth it does not come from your heart.

It is a "put on" smile. A genuine smile starts with your eyes and feels quite different. It does not feel like a reflex. It feels like love.

Try again.

Self-test 112: Touch a Tree—How Much has your Pleasure Grown?

A Zen story tells of a Master escorted on horseback to the emperor's palace. They had traveled long when finally the palace came in view. The guides sped forward but the Master kept his pace. "This is good too," he said.

What made the difference between Master and guides?

Awareness made the difference. When aware, satisfaction is complete.

Repeat: Touch a Tree (Self-test 56, Chapter Six). When you do you should now be reluctant to move on to the next thing. Lying under the tree watching sun filter through its leaves should be ecstasy. How much has your pleasure grown.

Self-test 113: Could You Be Happy Alone?

Could you be happy alone?

In full awareness, loneliness is impossible. As Thoreau said: "Why should I feel lonely, is not our planet in the Milky Way?"

Check again. See if you understand the broadest meaning of union. Could you be happy alone?

Self-test 114: Can You See the Miracle?

The Zen Master said: "Miracle of miracles! I carry water. I chop wood." He did not want his chores to be over with.

Pick a chore that is part of your routine: making coffee, writing checks, sorting laundry. Observe the habitual mental noise. Sorting laundry it might be: "darks...lights...lights...darks...lights..." Now stop the noise and be awed by the feel of textures, warmth and coolness of colors and soft soothing sounds. Experience the miracle and "get it over with" will not be your approach to life.

Self-test 115: A Riddle

Here is a riddle: When I am nothing, I am everything.

Does it make sense?

(Try reading it as: When I am nothing but awareness, I am everything.)

Self-test 116: Do You Understand the Question?

Irv Weinstein was a popular local newscaster. One day his four-year-old grandson asked: "Grandpa, if you didn't do the news on TV, would you still be Irv Weinstein?"

Does the question make sense to you?

The child wondered which was real: the living presence or the media image. The child of four was aware enough to see that there was a difference, to see through the mask. Only later in life is image everything.

Self-test 117: True and Useful?

A legendary Master spoke no word unless it passed two tests: Is it true? Will it help the listener?

Are you aware enough to witness; to know if what you are saying is true and useful?

Self-test 118: Grateful all the Time?

Imagine discovering an exotic wildflower of great beauty growing in your back yard. It would seem like a special gift, something over and above. You would be naturally grateful for it.

When aware, small wonders never seen before appear every day. The commonplace is like that flower, over and above. You will know you are aware if you are grateful all the time.

Self-test 119: Are you Lured toward the Goal?

When you practice, are you lured toward the goal?

A "yes" answer means inspiration has replaced desperation.

When you practice however, do not be lured by a vision of enlightenment. Be *propelled* by the force of attention so strongly that nothing could keep you from your goal.

Self-test 120: Is your Happiness Unconditional?

When Ram Dass was a barefoot yogi in India, his train was two days late and he had to wait in the station. It was crowded with people living there; vendors; goats and chickens; noise and confusion. The latrine had backed up days before. Raw sewage was everywhere and he had dysentery. He knew that everything in his background prepared him to be unhappy here, yet he was happy. This was real happiness, unconditional happiness, the kind that comes free: continuous outflow from an open heart.

Is your happiness unconditional?

Self-test 121: Vanishing Problems?

As you correct and balance yourself, the whole world is righted. Big problems get smaller. Some disappear.

Einstein said you can not solve a problem on the same level it was created. You have to rise to the next level. The next level is always broader awareness; higher vistas with bigger pictures. When you see why things should be as they are, problems dematerialize like clouds before the sun.

Are your problems vanishing?

Self-test 122: Test Your Understanding of Happiness.

People search for happiness by looking for love. Ask yourself: Can another person bring you happiness?

The answer is "yes, but…"

Happiness does not come from them loving you but from you loving them. The opportunity to love and so true happiness is always available. Take advantage of the opportunity and pursuit of happiness ends.

Self-test 123: Seeing What Is There?

Can you see what is there?

When a car drives toward you, the image the eye receives grows larger. This is not what you see however. The mind knows that the size of the car does not change, so size is held constant.

Awareness lets you see the image the eye actually receives. Move your hand slowly toward your face. Can you see the size of your hand increase? (Do not worry about images confusing you. At this practice level you are not easily confused.)

Self-test 124: Are you Prepared?

Think of the worst thing that could happen.

Are you prepared?

Self-test 125: Can you "remain unmoving until the right action arises by itself?"

The fascinating little book, *Zen and the Art of Archery* (Herrigel, 1953), tells of the author's training with a Master archer. We learn that the objective is not just hitting the target. The real target is a state of being in which the archer lets the arrow fly with no self-conscious effort. (A Master who hit a bull's eye in total darkness said: "I deserve no credit. I allowed 'something' to happen in me. This 'something' allowed the arrows to use the bow in order to join with the target.")

If you practice archery, play golf, bowl, etc, try this. See if you can do as Lao Tzu taught: "remain unmoving till the right action arises by itself." This action will be selfless, arising from pure awareness. (Chances are you have already passed this test with no self-congratulations.)

Self-test 126: Always Right?

My little girl heard my husband disagree with me. "Don't argue with Mommy, Daddy," she said. "Can't you see that she's always right?"

Appearing right does not mean having all the answers. It comes from awareness of uncertainty where uncertainty exists. This prevents error. When you speak it comes from bottomed-out certainty. Keeping silent, you might appear to be always right.

Self-test 127: Can You See What You Are?

Find a quiet place in your yard, in a park or botanical garden. Surrounded by beauty, repeat silently: "I'm looking at my face in the mirror...I'm looking at my face in the mirror..."

Can you see truth in this? Can you see there is more to you than you have ever imagined?

Self-test 128: Are you Still Running the Age Program?

A Karate student doing a move with difficulty said: "I'm getting old." Master Deac (age seventy-six and full of youthful strength and energy) responded: "We don't allow that here." He meant do not succumb to the concept of "old age."

How obedient are you to the age concept? Are you still running the program; harboring expectations, following deterioration guidelines? Here are some telltale signs:

Assuming some actual change occurs on your birthday.

Telling yourself: "I'm still young." (The program rattles on here too.)

Labeling how you feel as "young" or "old" (rather than "energetic"or "tired," for instance.)

Seeing people die of old age.

These are some signs of not running the program:

Willingness at any age to plant a tree.

Thinking of chronological age as mainly a handy ID tag.

Seeing gray hair as loss of pigmentation (not loss of youth).

Feeling as "at one" with persons in nursing homes as in nursery schools.

And most telling of all: Seeing the glow in your eyes that matches your baby pictures.

Master Deac says if his "feet don't skid" when he gets out of bed each morning something is wrong. An Army hospital recently called him in for an overnight stay. He was examined, monitored and questioned for hours on the resistance to aging seen in his mental sharpness, appearance, activity and in muscle tissue assessed as that of someone less than half his age. "How old are you," the Doctor asked as he was leaving. "Maybe late thirties" was his answer. Master Deac breaks all the rules, defies all the program's specifications.

Spring the conceptual trap and the age specter vanishes. The passage of time only fills you with more of your mansion's riches.

Self-test 129: The "Finer Things?"

Earlier you conjured an image of "a guy who really knows how to live," a picture perhaps of self-indulgence. Now conjure another image: "the finer things in life."

What do you see?

Is it different from what you thought these things were in the past?

At this practice level it might be radically different.

We tie up our hands clutching coins and jewelry when we could touch the stars. When awareness reveals the finer things, self-gratification resounds with emptiness.

Self-test 130: Changing Dream-life?

The work of dreams is problem solving. As you go you will have less need of this, and more peaceful sleep.

Birth into the world of peace and ease ends the need for problem solving altogether. You will awaken as if born in that instant: *all there* with no fog to disperse, no coming back from dreamland.

Do you notice a change in dream-life?

Self-test 131: Did you Wake up *Alive?*

Did you wake up *alive* this morning? Did you wake up to 3D and surround sound? Did you sense body movement as you arose and feel the carpet when your foot touched the floor? Were there thousands of tiny pelts of water droplets in your shower? Stepping outside, did you sense changes in the light and air? Was a sparrow as beautiful as a peacock; a dewdrop magnificent as the sea?

Being alive can feel very good.

Did you wake up *aware?*

Self-test 132: Do you want to Change Something?

How long has it been since you wanted to change someone or something?

Full awareness sees that everything is as it should be. "And all shall be well, and all shall be well, and all manner of thing shall be well." Nothing is more liberating than not needing to change a thing (and yet awareness is our strongest force for positive change).

Self-tests 133—136: Mirror Focusing Exercises *

Self-tests 133 through 136 have no right or wrong answers but are explorations of awareness. Sit a foot or two from a mirror and focus on the tip of your nose or the pupil of one eye. Feedback comes in the form of distortions of your face.

Self-test 133: Mirror Focusing: Are you Self-conscious? *

Do the distortions distress you?

Distress is a sign of self-consciousness. It means you are not ready for this exercise. Come back when the distortions do not bother you.

Self-test 134: Mirror Focusing: Constructing Reality? *

Focus on the distortions in the mirror. Notice how a slight change in mood influences what you see. A negative mood brings a negative image. What does this say about how your thinking mind distorts your world?

Self-test 135: Mirror Focusing: Seeing What You *Are Not.* *

Look at your face in the mirror. Repeat silently: "I am not that. I am not that."

With pure, impartial awareness, you will see you are not the image in the mirror but much, much more.

Self-test 136: Mirror Focusing: Seeing What You Are. *

Focus on the distortions and in time you may see faces. They will be faces of women and men, all races, all ages. Does this speak to you of what you are?

Self-test 137: Has "the Treasure" Spoken?

Tibetan tradition sees enlightenment as treasure buried under a poor man's house. The man lives in poverty and the treasure never says: "I'm here."

Restore awareness however, and your treasure *will* speak. Beauty will say "I'm here." It will announce itself even in the stairwell at the office and in the concrete under your feet. In full awareness, a crystalline purity pervades everything, even the garbage swarming with flies. The treasure speaks too in the night's ocean of cricket song; in sounds of shimmering poplars. Even as I write on this rainy autumn night, diamonds dance on the wire beneath my streetlight.

Has your treasure spoken?

Self-test 138: For whom are you Practicing?

In Chapter Nine I suggested you practice for someone else. For whom are you practicing?

Ultimately you will not be doing this for yourself. You will not be doing it for a single person either, or even for a group. At the highest level, no one will be excluded from your favor.

<u>Self-test 139: Is Your View "as Vast as the Sky?"</u>
How much has your perspective broadened? Have you seen a big picture?

Broad awareness sees infinite cause and effect connections. Can you trace the events that brought you to this book? When your view is "as vast as the sky" you will see why your reading this was meant to be.

<u>Self-test 140: Can you see Life's Bottom Line?</u>
There is a bottom line to life. Can you see what it is?

If you are getting a big picture you will see that the spiritual is life's bottom line.

<u>Self-test 141: Are you past "Trying?"</u>
My little girl understood effortless action. "You don't have to 'try' Mommy," she said, "just do it." She knew trying was unnecessary and unwise.

Awareness never tries. Without trying to do the right thing, the right thing emerges spontaneously. Without trying to be brave you are fearless. Without trying to use force you are powerful. Without trying to control things they come to perfection.

Are you past trying?

<u>Self-test 142: Finding Guidance?</u>
At this practice level you can always find guidance. Awareness sees what Whitman called "letters from God." "I find them dropt in the street," he wrote, "and I leave them where they are, for I know that whereso'er I go, others will punctually come for ever and ever (*Song of Myself*)."

Our souls are weak from starvation. Finding guidance through awareness your soul will find strength.

<u>Self-test 143: The "Problem person?" (I)</u>
Self-test 54 (Chapter Six) asked if there was a problem person in your life. You were asked to hold his head in your hands and gaze into his eyes.

Can you do this now? Can you see this problem person as your guide? Can you see in his eyes his innermost nature? Can you love? Can you thank him from the bottom of your heart?

Self-test 144: A Test of Happiness.

Remember taking your turn at a game, say, shooting baskets. If you did well, when your turn ended, you were content to stop. If you did poorly, you wanted another turn.

It is the same with life. Ask yourself: If it had to be, could you give up your turn now with contentment?

This is a test of true happiness.

Self-test 145: Are You Done With the Stopwatch?

Have you discontinued use of the stopwatch?

When the stopwatch becomes nothing more than a distraction, you have perfect concentration.

Self-test 146: Remembering you are Happy?

A strange realization can occur in awareness. It is remembering you are happy.

Coming to awareness can feel like waking from a troubled dream surprised to find that you are safe at home and on vacation. Have you felt such happiness?

Self-test 147: "Can You See With Your Ear?"

Ask yourself this: "Is consciousness in your head?"

As children we are taught that we think with our brains, see with our eyes and hear with our ears. These concepts are poor representations of actual experience. Awareness reveals the astonishing truth. Consciousness is not in your head.

Zen asks: "Can you see with your ear?"

Self-test 148: How Many Hearts?

It is said that everyone has three hearts. One is shown to the world. The second is for close friends and family, and the third is private. It is your heart of hearts, known only to yourself.

How many hearts do you have?

With full awareness it is only one, the third, your heart of hearts, and it will be for everyone.

Self-test 149: Are you Looking Up?

Master Deac said of Master Choe: "I'm not perfect. *He* was." Perhaps Choe said the same of himself in relation to his teacher MoKow, and MoKow of TiLe and so forth.

Real happiness comes with humility. It comes from looking up, not down. To a big me everything looks small.

I work to clear my self away, to be nothing but awareness. When I feel humble before a blade of grass I can look up and see greatness in all people, beauty in the commonplace and the perfection in the grand design.

Can you look up high enough to see perfection? Can you be humble before a blade of grass?

Self-test 150: "Yes!" to Everything?

If a jury duty summons came in the mail today, how would you react?

An emphatic "Yes!" means you are present in your mansion.

"Yes!" to everything means going in the direction of the Plan. Even a jury duty summons holds something for you.

Self-test 151: What do you like to do Most?

If you could choose anything, what would you like most to do?

A wise answer is: "loving," because it is what humans do best. Loving engages full human capacity, maximum power of awareness, and loving brings true happiness.

Recheck your Love Tests answers (page 61) and see how you have changed.

Self-test 152: Have you found the Path?

Do you feel you have found the path?

If so, go deeper into awareness. You may reach a point where you see no path, no distance you have covered and no position you stand in now.

Paths are concepts. They can be useful direction finders but they are still noise in your head. You can be freer.

Self-test 153: The Hour Hand. *

You saw the minute hand move in Chapter Six (Self-test 53). Now try the hour hand.

Seeing the hour hand move takes concentration of breakthrough intensity. When you see it move you will be in the neighborhood of ninety-five percent awareness, five percent noise.

(Focusing on the hour hand is an excellent exercise even if no movement is seen. Attend to the minute hand afterward and you will easily see its movement. This proves your awareness has grown.)

Self-test 154: Loss of Faith?

As the Zen story goes a farmer's only son fell and broke his leg. Everyone saw it as tragic. Then soldiers came to take the young man off to war. They left him home because of the injury and he survived.

Next the farmer's only horse ran away. Everyone saw it as tragic. Days later the horse returned with several wild horses, and on the story goes.

Faith is another of your mansion's halls. If you are present there you will know why negative judgment in this story was faithless. Awareness, the well-spring of faith, sees the Divine hand in everything.

Do you have faith? Pause here and ask yourself what you would do if you lost it?

Handle this just as you handle other doubts. Use your practice. Get clear enough and faith will be restored. You need only eyes to see.

Self-test 155: Too Much Beauty?

At this practice level you might find beauty overwhelming. If you do you are still disconnected from what is there, separate and judgmental. It is your judgment, not the beauty that overwhelms you.

Go further with your practice and *be* the beauty. Then the problem ends.

Self-test 156: Mysterious Tears?

You might experience tears neither of joy or sadness. They might be tears for former pain now being resolved. If you experience this, ask whose pain is it you cry for?

Is it yours?

Is it someone else's?

With enough awareness you will see that there is no difference.

Self-test 157: Have you changed your Mind Lately?

How long has it been since you changed your mind?

As awareness grows you will change your mind less. This is because you do not "make up your mind" in the first place.

Thinking always teeters on the next thought. Awareness rests in certainty. When awareness is your locus of control you will know by means of awareness (not by thoughts that err). You will act out of awareness (not blindly out of concepts).

How sure are you?

Have you stopped changing your mind?

Self-test 158: Where are You?

Where are you?

When aware, the answer to this question is always the same. Traveling far, you never leave home. The answer is always "I am here; I am present."

Master Deac teaches that you should stay centered. When you see a passing car, for instance, you should not be moving along the street with it. You should be still and present, centered here now.

Look out in the street and test yourself for centeredness, for presence.

Self-test 159: A Listening Test.

The visually impaired may find this test of awareness especially useful.

Focus on the tick of a clock or metronome. Is the tick:

Not heard at all?

Heard in the background of thoughts?

Heard in the foreground of thoughts?

Heard as the ground of being with no thoughts at all?

Low awareness hears little or no ticking. You hear only your thoughts.

Moderate awareness hears ticking in the background, on and off.

High awareness hears the sound in the foreground of experience.

Full awareness makes the sound "the ground of being," the base or bottom part over which other parts lie. In full awareness there is no listener. You have become the sound. This is at-one-ment.

Self-test 160: What are you Living For?

Ask yourself: "What am I living for?"

Do you have an answer?

If so, is it known through awareness or did you think it up?

If you thought it up, do not trust it absolutely.

If it is known through awareness, rest in it.

If you have no answer, that is okay. Do not trouble your mind.

Self-test 161: What kind of a Person are You?

If someone asked: What kind of person are you, would you have trouble answering?

If you would you pass this test. It means you do not see yourself in it.

Go on until you wear no mask, until your personal history does not constrain what you are. Then you will be at your best.

Self-test 162: Which Are You?

At the highest level of awareness are you:

a) Great as the greatest of all time?

b) Equal to the humblest creature on earth?

When aware enough to see human perfection, you also see how arrogant and foolish it would be to think of yourself as perfect. (In time the contradiction will not bother you at all.)

Self-test 163: No Difference?

Take your exercise outside. Focus on sounds around you: a bird's song, a breeze, etc. Concentrate and repeat silently: "There is no difference between me and…(a bird's song, the breeze, etc.)."

Now ask yourself: Is it true? Is there *no* difference between you and what you are aware of?

Remember what Toscanini told musicians: "Abandon yourself to the music." Abandon yourself and you are your target. There is no difference between you and what you are aware of. Then you are truly free.

Self-test 164: Have you seen Oneness? (I)

Have you seen oneness?

Try this in imagination. Put yourself in another world, a world with no eyes so you have no vision. Now take away hearing. You have no ears:

the world is soundless. Now take away the sense of touch: no skin, no feelers. Holding this in mind, can you imagine yourself as *separate* from others?

If you have a good imagination, you have just glimpsed oneness. Of course this is only a mental trick. Go on until no one is there who has any interest in sensing oneness.

Self-test 165: A Higher Standard?

Beginners measuring success ask: "Do I feel better now? Is my mind quieter?" Success is relative, a matter of degree.

At the highest level success becomes absolute.

This is because when you scale this high peak you are *all* there. The measure of success at this level is: Am I present or absent? Am I awake or not?

How advanced is your practice? Is your standard relative or absolute?

Self-test 166: Are you Still a Visitor?

Do you feel like a visitor passing through life?

I once felt like a visitor, but I found this to be an illusion.

Awareness sees no visit and no visitor. On the contrary, it sees that you have never left home and nowhere that is not home could possibly exist.

This sense of belonging is the experience of union. You are far more at home in this life than the thinking mind can begin to grasp.

Self-test 167: The "End of Suffering?"

Try this next time you have a minor ache or pain, at the dentist for instance. See if you can be at one with it.

It is possible in physical pain not to judge it as "my pain." What makes something unbearable is the need to escape it. Suffering ends when resistance ends. That is why singing the blues (being one with the pain), cures the blues.

When in pain, can you be this free? Can you refrain from judgment? Can you experience an "end of suffering" right in the middle of it?

Self-test 168: Is Your Pool Guarded?

How long has it been since you said: "*That* got me mad," or "*They* made me afraid," or "*He* upset me?"

By now you have awareness enough to see that no one but you can make you upset. Through lapse of awareness you allow others to throw pebbles in your pool, and through lapse of awareness you throw them in yourself. Awareness alone keeps you clear and cool.

How well is your pool guarded?

Self-test 169: Can you *always* be a Giver and a Non-taker?

The sage said "Always be a giver and a non-taker." Is it *always* possible?

Suppose you ask your boss for a raise. Can you still be a giver and a non-taker?

If you are aware you can be. You will be giving in your willingness to serve; giving in your wish to care for loved ones; giving through empathy in knowing you are distressing the boss. All of these signify outflow of love. Even asking for a raise you can be a giver.

Self-test 170: Your Most Important Experience?

Look back on your life. What was your most important experience?

If you have learned life's lessons, your most painful experience might well be the most important and valued of your life. It may have proven to be the seed of a great tree.

Self-test 171: Do You "Know Without Knowing?"

"How did you know that?" the Karate Master asks.

"I don't know," replies the student.

"Then you have reached the highest level," says the Master.

In Chinese martial tradition, at the highest level you "know without knowing." Christian mystics describe this too: "you know without knowing how you know." This is the feel of pure awareness. I felt it when predicting the weather without being able to identify any cues.

Is there something you know without knowing how you know?

Self-test 172: Would you have "Wandered and Thirsted?"

Master Choe and his disciple went on a dangerous mission behind enemy lines spying out the source of the enemy's supply of ammunition. Deep in enemy territory they discovered camouflaged foot soldiers carrying munitions. They radioed back the location and began their return.

As they traveled the young soldier became thirsty. Finding a brook he lay down and cupped water as silently as he could from his palm to his mouth. They went on.

At a safer distance Master Choe said: "You have endangered my life this day." Deac wore a confused look. "You left here," said Master Choe. He told him he had wandered, drifted to thoughts of home and thirsted. The disciple had done exactly that.

The Master however, even with the mission accomplished, did not break from awareness. "The calm" was his normal resting state.

Would you have "wandered and thirsted?"

"Aware presence," as Master Choe said, "will save your life and it will save your soul."

Self-test 174: Feeling Selfless?

Do you feel selfless?

If you feel selfless you are surely not. A better test of selflessness comes in Corinthians (13:4-8):

> Love is patient, love is kind, it does not envy, it does not boast, it is not proud. It is not rude, it is not self-seeking, it is not easily angered, it keeps no record of wrongs. Love does not delight in evil but rejoices with the truth. It always protects, always trusts, always hopes, always perseveres. Love never fails.

These are the qualities of selflessness. Are you looking at your face in the mirror?

Self-test 175: How Good was your Day?

Zen says: "Every day is a good day." How good was today?

Would you welcome re-living it over and over and over for all time, or would you want tomorrow to be different in some way?

When you would gladly relive today *eternally* you have arrived. Not until then. That is how good a day can be.

Self-test 176: A Goal of Your Own?

Several years ago I set a goal. I hoped that when someone looked in my eyes, that person could see what they are. I still aspire to this.

Is there some point you want to reach; some challenge you want to meet? Make it a Self-test tailored for you. Set a goal and see how you measure up.

<u>Self-test 177: Holding the Key to Happiness?</u>

When I was very young I found the key to happiness in *Cinderella*. Through all her trials my storybook said: "She grew in love and goodness." This allowed her to forgive, and it made all creatures her intimates. I wanted to grow in love and goodness. I gave this a lot of thought as a child, but I could not see how to do it and I left the dream behind. Now I know what it takes. As we saw before, without awareness it is impossible to love. With it, it is impossible not to.

The mountain range represented in Advanced Self-tests is vast, and you may find that you can scale these peaks and later find yourself again at sea level. Love and goodness however, are constant when you realize your true nature. Maintain awareness and you hold this key and you are protected and sustained in all things.

This concludes advanced Self-tests. Pass them and you have mastered the master skill. Now you can "rouse the wind and stir the grasses." A breakthrough is at hand.

CHAPTER ELEVEN
BREAKTHROUGH!

Astonish heaven and shake the earth!
Mumon

This chapter helps you penetrate the last of the barrier, to "pass through the silver mountain and the iron wall." Before starting however, I'd like to share my breakthrough experience with you.

It happened over thirty years ago on the summer afternoon mentioned in Chapter One. Gazing at a spot I saw the light. My search for efficient meditation ended. I used the light as feedback and within an hour I broke through.

My memory of this day is still fresh. It was a Friday and I recall thinking: "I have the whole weekend...plenty of time." I knew it could be done and I determined to do it. Eagerly I focused in.

Within seconds a vibrant halo of light appeared around the spot. First a narrow band, it widened and spread very slowly the way the moon crosses the night sky.

I was aware of my surroundings: a clock's tick and noises from the street. These sounds were not distractions however. They were signal, not noise. Once or twice I said to myself: "On target...doing fine." That *was* noise, but it lasted only seconds. In forty-five minutes the room was filled with shimmering light.

I had read somewhere: "Go into the light," but I did no such thing. For me the light was receptor fatigue, important only as feedback, my anchor for attention. I held on.

My concentration was intense, my power contained. Earnings poured back into the business. Each minute built on the success of the last and the exercise gained its own momentum, propelling me on.

In Chapter Two I said inner gravity settles thoughts. Here intense concentration created the gravitational force of a black hole. The whole pyramidal structure of mind, from the little chatterbox on top to the broad unconscious base was sucked in, receding so far that no thought could possibly escape. I came to full power and hovered there, poised on the threshold of infinity, about to erase eons of errors of mind.

Then on its own it came. It seemed even unrelated to my efforts. It was not like a balloon popping from explosive force. As others have described it, with a sense of dawning it came silently: "Something's different," I thought, and it was there.

There was a lightening-fast return to a single cell in my mother's womb, and within her to her mother's womb, and from there to her mother's, and so back and back and back and back and back and back before recorded time, back to the primordial ooze and still further to the Big Bang, and there finding myself its chief engineer...

It was as if that happened because what else could afford this perspective on infinity? Timelessly, agelessly, without place or position, I became *what is*.

They say a gateless barrier separates you from what you really are. If you are moving fast when you hit the barrier you soar through, and deep, deep within you linger with ultimate answers. What is God? What is death? What is the meaning of life? What of human learning? Eternity is at your fingertips and you can dip in and draw forth knowledge.

The word "transcend" to describe this (as in Transcendental Meditation) is misleading. It turns out we have been transcending all along without knowing it. We have been on the mezzanine thinking we are on the ground floor. Breakthrough corrects this. You do not 'rise above.' Awareness grounds you. Where once you were a blind man trying to see an elephant, now you *are* the elephant. And it is not an intuition you have had. It is union with the source of intuition, and it is not so "mystical" as crystal clear.

"Ten suns shining"

Constant thinking blocks awareness as ever-present clouds block the sun. When darkness is constant however, we do not know we are in darkness. This makes the light of awareness seen at breakthrough startling. Everything is transparent, "distinctly clear as if there were ten suns shining (in Cleary, 1978, page 71)." All philosophical problems, (mind-body problems included), are resolved by being shown to have no reason to exist. They were mental corners we painted ourselves into with words. Full awareness springs the trap, ending confusion and illusion. You see all the way to the bottom, clear through misunderstandings you never even knew were misunderstandings, like the one concerning what you are. You see not who but *what* you are. You see what you are and you are what you see. You see the complete unadorned, unadornable you. The ugly duckling disappears and a swan's mighty wingspan unfolds in Great Knowledge.

- Great Knowledge

Of the many facets of enlightenment, Great Knowledge had the most draw for me. I needed to know.

My parents worked hard to afford a house in the suburbs. Before the interior was finished, my father died suddenly of a heart attack. My mother died of cancer several years later. No day of my young life passed without a heartfelt "Why?" I looked for answers in books but the more I learned the greater seemed the depth of my ignorance. Since breakthrough however, no single "Why" has troubled me. I found answers in "an inner core of light and intelligence as vast as ten thousand worlds (Lenz, 1995, page 25.)." All of these answers were beyond words.

As a way of knowing, awareness makes "books, scriptures, and science appear as mere dirt and straw (Sri Ramakrishna, 1985, page 21)." We are wrong in thinking words are knowledge. The error stems from the disconnection Whitman described. "When I heard the learn'd astronomer," he wrote:

> When the proofs, the figures, were ranged in columns before me...
> How soon unaccountable I became tired and sick, Till rising and gliding out
> I wander'd off by myself, in the mystical moist night air, and from time to
> time, Look'd up in perfect silence at the stars.

Words distance and separate us from the stars. Awareness communes with their essence. We believe *thinking* is knowing, but *being* is knowing. Be what is and "To glance with an eye confounds the learning of all time."

Great knowledge knows how to be; how to live; how to be happy. Right actions arise from awareness as naturally as maples shed leaves. Right action, as Molinos described it: "isn't contrived or studied but flows spontaneously, just as it comes from purity and simplicity of heart." No decision is made here; no principle referred to.

Master Choe said: be consistent with reality. With awareness:

The view of reality as it is becomes his right view. Thought of reality as it is becomes his right thought. Effort toward reality as it is becomes his right effort...Actions of body and speech become truly purified (Buddha, in Hart, 1987, page 156).

In awareness you know what to do in the same way a bird knows which way to fly in the spring. The bird knows because he is not asking: "I wonder which way is north?" He does not need to think because he is not on the outside out of touch. He is fused, one.

We plot and plan direction. Awareness needs no thought or plan. When you are one with everything you do not wonder which way to go. You go freely and sure-footedly the right way just like the bird. The Chauffeur automatically knows which way to turn.

Low awareness limits contact with reality. Our problem is we do not know our contact with reality is limited. Dairy products have a 'real' symbol so we can be sure we are not getting something man-made. In life however, man-made, mind-made things pass as real. Zen *koans*, like "the sound of one hand clapping," pose problems that are not real but mind-made, problems that could not exist without thoughts to confuse us. Only awareness can furnish answers for these problems; only awareness knows what is real. The same is true of the problem of the meaning of life.

The Meaning of Life?

The meaning of life is not a real problem either. It is mind-made, invented by a puzzle maker lost in thought. He veiled life in uncertainty the way a film of paint covers a crystal ball. The puzzler however, unaware he was lost in a maze of ideas, did not know he had invented the problem: did not know the trouble was only the veil of uncertainty.

The meaning of life is noise in the system. Remember the centipede:

...happy quite, until a toad in fun, said 'pray, which leg goes after which?'
This worked his mind to such a pitch he lay distracted in a ditch considering
how to run.

Considering how to run...

When we puzzle over life's meaning we are considering how to run. Looking for principles to base our lives on shows a "which leg goes after which" problem, a monkey-wrench in the works. It is like a bird wondering which way to fly in the spring, quite lost, as we are.

The solution is to stop the questioning, to stop the noise. Only in silence does the swan soar free. Only in awareness do you *live* life's meaning, and know you are life's meaning, its whole meaning.

When aware you rest in truth. There is no need to puzzle. You do not have to think if you know. You are through puzzling when you see all the pieces perfectly in place, all moving in unison in exquisite order, each determining the exact position of all others.

Thoreau went alone to the woods to know life. He wanted:

...to live deliberately...to live deep...to reduce life to its lowest terms. For most men, it appears to me, are in a strange uncertainty about it.

Awareness resolves our "strange uncertainty" when meaning is seen through clear eyes. When all the noise is stilled and the tenant evicted, the film peels away from the crystal ball and meaning shines out to light the world.

Words are inventions. Truth is not. Know that which is not words. Be a lion with a golden mane. Be yourself.

Now for the how to of breakthrough.

How to Break Through

Before beginning you should understand where you are going. What does it mean to be "one with everything?" Master Choe's words convey its meaning.

In martial arts, the Master-disciple bond can be stronger than family ties. Such a bond formed between Master Choe and his disciple in Korea. Later the army facilitated their venture, stationing both men at Fort Lewis. After seven years together, time came for final parting. "Why was I chosen," asked Master Deac? "You are the brother I never had, the laughter I never knew," said Choe. "On my best day I will remember you, and on my worst day it will bring me back." Both men knew they would never meet again. Choe, sensing his disciple's unease, spoke these parting words: "On some pleasant day," he said, "you will feel a comforting breeze on your cheek. I feel this too, or will on the morrow."

Master Choe's parting words embody the essence of enlightenment: we *are one*. All facets of the multifaceted jewel arise from this union. To be "one with everything" is to have Great Liberation, Great Knowledge, Great Tranquility and Great Love.

How do you become one with everything?

It works like this. First attention quiets the mind until nothing blocks awareness. This brings contact with reality, but what if you do not stop building awareness? What if you continue on?

Remember Groucho's line? His dance partner said "Hold me closer, closer!" Groucho said: "If I were any closer I'd be behind you." You can get just so close to something. Then, if you keep moving forward, something has to give. What happens if you push further into contact with reality? The answer is fusion. You fuse with reality. You become one with everything. How is this done? Let's define the task.

- Defining the Task

Have you ever had a mouse in your house? Looking for its entry you may have found a hole that seemed too small, but he *did* pass through it.

You have to do here what that mouse did. You have to squeeze through a tiny opening. It is so small you can not fit through carrying anything. You can not get through holding opinions or bearing grudges. There is no room for emotion or doubt that you will succeed. Even a wish for enlightenment must be left behind. In fact the hole is so infinitesimal there is no opening whatsoever. This is not a problem however, because there is no wall there either.

When you downsize to nothing, nothing is there to impede you. You see that the wall you have been trying to penetrate does not exist. You see it never has existed, and that the notion of "contact with reality" is really quite absurd. How after all could you possibly be outside of reality?

Still you must downsize to break through. Here are some guidelines for peak performance.

Guidelines for Peak Performance

Ask yourself: How forceful would concentration have to be for you to "overturn the sky and wrap up the earth?"

How deep would silence have to be for you to find something in yourself that was there before your birth?

This is the force and depth of concentration needed to break through. Toy with this breakthrough and you will only be discouraged. If you want to take the challenge however, these guidelines can help.

Build Confidence with the Self-tests. They say that when Buddha determined to reach enlightenment an evil spirit tried to tempt him from his goal. There were violent winds and firestorms to frighten him, beautiful women to seduce him away, but he held his course.

In a final attempt to stop him the spirit said: "Who are you to think that you can be enlightened?" Buddha touched the ground and the earth shook in confirmation. This is how certain you can feel.

How can you feel this certain? Go back and prove yourself with the Self-tests.

Sit Better. Picture yourself at your kitchen table. Someone hands you a puzzle and says solve this in one minute for ten thousand dollars. How does your posture change?

Duplicate this change when you sit down to practice. Use what a Zen Master called: "strategic action of the whole capacity."

Build Power Over Time. When the noisy tenant is not draining you, energy builds and is contained. This energy can deploy as physical power, moral power, healing power, creative power, etc. Here we are using it to see clearly. For this you must build power over time.

A weight lifter out to break a record trains daily building to peak performance. Build your concentration in this way. Learn to hold attention the way a weight lifter lifts weights, delivering what is needed on demand.

Don't Let Down. Breakthroughs follow energy build ups. While you attend, energy builds behind a dam of silence. Feedback tells you the dam is in place. When energy builds to a critical threshold you have fusion.

A teacher in martial tradition advised that we meditate until we see and feel nothing but our own energy. Two factors lead to such energy buildup: advanced practice skill and *not letting down.*

This is like rubbing sticks together to start a fire, what counts is not the number of minutes, but the number of consecutive minutes. Stop to rest and you start again cold. Continuous attention lets no energy escape, so don't let down.

Now for some tips on peak performance.

Tips for Peak Performance

- ### Know You Can Do It

A professor I had in college told about helping his daughter with math. One question in her book had a star in the margin indicating difficulty and he could not solve it. The next day he shared it with colleagues, telling them it was difficult. They could not get it either. As soon as he put it aside however, the solution came to him. With no aura of difficulty, it was easy. Difficulty was created by expectation alone.

Unfortunately enlightenment has a big star in the margin that shakes our confidence. You can counter expectations of difficulty by understanding exactly how attention focusing practice works, and why feedback guarantees success.

The lesson of simplicity applies here. Attention creates awareness pure and simple. Awareness sees truth pure and simple. The feat you perform here is simply that of seeing what is before your eyes. So forget "enlightenment." Just be as aware as you were born. You are unthinkably close to full awareness. The barrier is as thin as microscopic ice.

Know that if you came yard one, you can go the final yard because it covers the same ground. Do not handicap yourself with notions of difficulty. Forget difficult and forget easy too. Not doing it is the only way to fail.

- ### Don't Wait for Luck

Some meditation teachers tell students: With luck you'll break through. Know that luck is not necessary. The task is attention, razor sharp, single-minded, performed with the conviction you can not fail. You need only practice skill and single-minded purpose. These are in your hands so do not wait for luck.

• Don't Stop to Wonder

Wondering if something is about to happen will stop you cold. Remember, feedback means you are going in a straight line. The goal is straight ahead, so if you go long enough you can not help getting there.

Don't stop to wonder. Hold ground dead center.

• Hold Ground Dead Center

A breakthrough does not take you somewhere over the rainbow. It restores you to the here and now. If you find yourself lost in a dream of oneness remember you are still lost. Do not drift away. Stay where you exist as awareness and nothing else. Hold ground dead center. Straight-line meditation takes you straight through.

• Keep Awareness Pure

Let me explain why pure awareness is your aim.

If you were in a foxhole watching for the enemy, concentration would be intense. The need to kill or be killed however, would pollute your awareness.

Do not pollute awareness with a need to be enlightened. You can not be at one if part of you is tied up elsewhere. As Master Deac says: "Be your target." *Be* attention and awareness will be pure.

• Get Desperate

A seeker asked a Guru: "When will I see God?" The Guru led him to a lake, walked him in, thrust his head under and held it there. Then he released him, asking: "How did you feel?" "I thought I would die," said the man. "I needed to breathe!" "When you feel like that for God you will know you haven't long to wait," said the Guru.

Getting desperate helps. With inspiration and desperation you will do what it takes to get the job done. Put in the same effort it would take to burst into flame. Then you have not long to wait.

- ## Know it's There

Imagine you are adrift on the ocean in a boat. You need water, but you have searched the boat time and again and found none. Then, just sitting there, your foot strikes something beneath your seat. A jug of water has been there all along. Similarly, what you are seeking is already here *now*.

Physicist Marie Curie knew something was there though unseen. She spent months separating out components in tons of pitch-blend. When the job was done she had found nothing, so she ordered more ore and began again, painstakingly sifting through it. This time when she was done, glowing in the bottom of a vessel was radium, for which discovery she won the Nobel Prize.

Madame Curie succeeded because she persisted, and she persisted because she knew it was there. Be like this, not questioning how long it takes and never giving up because *you know it's there!*

Now consider some factors contributing to success.

Factors Contributing to Success

Aspiring writers asked a prominent author how to know if they were meant to write. He said: "If you wake up every day and start writing, you were meant to write." The same goes here. You will break through if you wake up each day and start working with single-minded purpose. Motivation is all-important.

Ample time is another factor contributing to success. The secure feel of adequate time helps you get down to business in earnest. But remember, feedback time, not practice time counts. Aim for quality first, then quantity. Feedback makes your journey the shortest distance between two points, a straight line to liberation.

Your experience of breakthrough will be as unique as you are. In mine I see four factors contributing to success: the guidance of feedback; a capacity for sustained attention; absolute confidence (I knew feedback guaranteed attention and therefore success), and strong motivation. Let me expand on these.

I had meditated energetically every day for several months before my breakthrough. With this I built a capacity for sustained attention. Advanced Self-tests will tell you if you have this capacity.

I was confident of a sure thing because I understood that feedback means attention, and attention inevitably zeros in to ultimate reality. I remember realizing: "If some 'enlightenment' is possible, *this* is the way there." You should have such confidence too.

Finally I had motivation. I wanted knowledge. I was also very strongly drawn to the "perfect mental balance" promised by tradition.

Develop practice skill. Know you have a sure thing. Stay motivated. Hold on to attention, and its all-systems-go.

Doing this you have set up conditions for something to happen on its own. Your hard climb will become an ascent. Your breakthrough will come in the fullness of time the way a ripe apple falls from a tree. Still it may be possible to estimate how long it will take once on target.

Hindu tradition says: "holding the mind unwaveringly for twelve seconds constitutes a meditation. Twelve of these—that is twelve such meditations in unbroken sequence brings breakthrough (Paramananda, 1982, page 44)." The term "unwavering" is a loose term here. Experience will teach you the difference between unwavering, and UNWAVERING! Aim to overshoot the mark.

Remember feedback is all you need. It is a pruning shears: the only tool you need to downsize. Limit your experience to feedback. Keep cutting back. Cutting back. Cutting back. Achieve a blank slate and then no slate at all. Wash away all that is not gold.

- <u>What Comes Next?</u>

At breakthrough, according to Zen, "you are like a dumb person who has had a wonderful dream, only he knows it personally within himself." After breakthrough, for a brief time I knew profound sanity, the higher standard discussed in Chapter Seven. For days I floated bodiless, fluid as air. Distress was impossible in any circumstance.

The sanity was absolute and so profound I thought I was set for life. I stopped practicing. Then one day (I recall the exact moment, entering my apartment, the key in my hand turning in the lock), I heard it again, the noise in my head. Some inane trifle was drawing me into the overlay, blocking my light. "Oh No," I said aloud. "It's back!"

Great Tranquility ebbs away. Great Knowledge however, stays.

A breakthrough is like an athletic peak performance. Afterward the athlete still has to work to maintain fitness. More than once over the years I have gone off course. I have made myself a nervous wreck and I have had bouts of major depression. I have never had to wonder how this happened however, and I have always known that awareness could have prevented it.

You can count on truth, on Great Knowledge like Olympic gold to stay with you. Your practice skill stays too. It remains your home ground and you can return to it at any time. And more good news: mysterious as it seems, no matter how complete your experience, there is infinitely more you can gain.

Expect to move in and out of awareness depending on the quality of your practice. It is best, after birth into the world of peace and ease to stay and grow there. Keep returning to the source. It will continue to draw you, and no matter how far you go, gains will never stop increasing.

A Zen Master advised:

even if you have an enlightenment, you must give up every enlightenment you realize and time and again return to the awakening host, go back to the fundamental; if you can guard it firmly...your inherent nature will become clear just as a jewel becomes more lustrous with polishing; eventually it will illumine worlds in all directions (Zen Master Bassui, in Cleary, 1978).

Now drop all expectations. If you are expecting anything you are not doing it. Just perform this simple act of radical reductionism. Subtract and subtract and subtract until it adds up to your salvation.

CHAPTER TWELVE
FACETS OF THE JEWEL

Conceive of nothing and I give you heaven.
Buddha, spoken through Jack Kerouac

In this Chapter several facets of the jewel are illustrated with experiences I have had in deep awareness. They exemplify guidance, awareness of truth and the power of love. Your experience may be completely unlike mine, still if you need inspiration I think you will find it here.

I was not alone in the pool. A small frog was at the far end frantically trying to escape me. I remembered a Zen story:

Why does the rabbit run from you, asks the Master?

Because he is afraid, says the student.

Because you have a killer instinct, says the Master.

Feeling ashamed of my killer instinct I watched the creature exhausting itself. Then suddenly, unexpectedly, all of my thoughts were gone. I entered the frog's domain, awareness. We were eye to eye and we shared an understanding. It was clearer and more complete than any communication I have ever had in words. We were of *one mind*. I stretched out my arms at the water's surface and the frog swam with strong sure strokes straight across the pool and into my open hands. I lifted it out and after a minute it hopped away.

My daughter saw this from a window and we shared a moment of silent awe. Then unexpectedly, a lesson came through as these words sounded in my head: "All concepts are barriers to truth: *even Zen Masters' concepts.*"

In that moment of communion with the frog I had full contact with reality; total freedom from concepts of frogs and instincts and of myself as separate. When I am this aware I find that guidance is woven into the fabric of my life.

I find such guidance most often outdoors. There I am most free, not living in my head, isolated from the natural world, missing the vibrant now. On visits to the woods I have learned many lessons. A few of these follow.

Guidance in the Corridors of Heaven

Near my home is Sprague Brook Park, a thousand acres of forest and meadow. There are pine, oak, thorn apple, ash, hickory, ironwood and maple trees. Apple and cherry blossoms color spring landscapes. Wild blackberries line mountain-bike trails, reminding me of Whitman's words: "and the running blackberry would adorn the corridors of heaven."

These tree-lined corridors are halls of learning for me. If I am aware there, every glint of sunlight and flicker of leaves has meaning of great depth. Guidance is present like air is, in and around me always. All creatures are my intimates, and birds, chipmunks and deer become my teachers. Once, an owl taught me.

An Owl's Confirmation

It was an autumn day in a troubled time for me. I wanted guidance and I was seeking it.

Passing by a brook I sensed I should stop. I did. As I stood by the water my attention was caught by a fallen maple leaf floating lightly along. I watched it swirl and dip with the current, gliding with effortless ease. I observed that it had no need to choose direction to get where it was going. It had no need to steer. There was no struggle to stay afloat and no need to paddle. An insight occurred to me: one's life could be that easy.

Wayne Dyer said True peace is: "not separating yourself from the will of God (*Inspiration*, 2006)." If my life were perfectly consistent with reality (one with the Plan), it would require no choice of direction; no steering; no struggle. Great Knowledge assures right thought and action. Action flows out of truth, as Master MoKow advised. The Chauffeur (not the trouble-making tenant) has the wheel. Awareness does everything. I realized that if I were flowing with this current, there would be *no need for guidance*; no need at all.

I stood awed by the insight when a great owl swooped down from behind me. It passed by so closely I felt wind from its wings on my face. It was gray; battle scarred, and it seemed dusty with age. The sight of it in the noonday sun astonished me. It flew up, lighted on a high branch and sat stone still facing me. I was transfixed by its large eyes. Then a single word sounded in me: "*Wisdom.*"

My insight was confirmed.

A Flower's Teaching

"I go and come with a strange liberty in nature," wrote Thoreau, "a part of herself." I know this liberty, and I know why it feels strange. It feels strange because when you are aware in the woods, *you are the woods.* You are not seeing what is there. You are being what is there.

When aware in the woods I see perfection in the positioning of every leaf and limb, in every clod and pebble. At such times I am not seeing perfection but being perfection, not seeing beauty but being beauty. Then "narrow shafts of Divine Light pierce the thin veil that separates heaven and earth." I walk in a dream, though I know I am not dreaming. The ecstasy of soul is beyond all pleasures of sense.

In this state of awareness, guidance flows continuously. Trees teach me lessons of the relativity of time and of the strength in silence. Brooks teach of eternity, directing me to go on and on unceasing. Once, a lavender wildflower taught me.

It stood as tall as I by the trail's side and easily caught my eye. Slowing my bike to see it, its wonderful fragrance stopped me. For days afterward, I revisited the flower every time I passed. Then one day I saw it was withering. "How sad," I thought. "It is the only one."

As I stood mourning its loss, another such flower in the bud caught my eye. Then behind that I saw another flower, and looking to my right and left I saw a hundred more. A forest of them was just starting to bloom. The lesson struck deep. Mourning the flower's end I had been confused. I was forgetting that *now will always be.*

Not Alone

When I am most aware, all woodland creatures are my teachers. Flowers, trees and brooks teach passively, simply by being what they are. Animals however, like the frog in my pool, teach actively, interacting with me in mysterious, wonderful ways.

Writing this book was very difficult for me and it was made more difficult by thinking I was alone in the work. In the woods I was taught otherwise.

One day I was met at the trail's entrance by a large doe. It leapt from the woods and crossed in front of me. Then to my wonderment it stayed with me running parallel to my trail, weaving in and out as I biked along. Half the time it was airborne, leaping high as if to convey to me its spectacular power and grace.

At the trail's end, hoping against hope that this enchantment might continue, I turned to make a second loop. The creature stayed with me! Then as I rode I found myself repeating: "I am not alone."

At the end where the trail opens on a meadow, the deer came close and crossed in front of me just as it had before. Seeing its coat I gasped. That day had been gray and cloudy, but just as the deer passed close before my eyes, a sunbeam on its coat spotlighted a flash of gold. The brilliant image will never be forgotten. I was not alone.

Help from Three Deer

If I have the union awareness creates, guidance in the woods is as continuous as breathing. Deer come out, fauns approach me and all of it has meaning and purpose. If I am not clear headed however, the deer hide. It seems they come out to teach only if they have a receptive student.

At the time this lesson was taught I was troubled by self-consciousness. Meeting people I was anxious: "What will they think of me? How do I look? Will I say the right thing?" The serene presence I knew so often in the woods was rarely mine in public and I wanted it. I knew it should be calm and loving, but when I tried to be calm and loving in public, I was more self-conscious (less present) than ever. How could I develop such presence I wondered as I biked along?

Soon I left these thoughts and awareness returned. The beauty all around me flowed in and I voiced a silent "thank you." Then I noticed something intriguing. At that thankful moment I was calm and loving. I had the very presence I sought, and the "thank you," the gratitude, was its source.

Could gratitude be a presence I could cultivate through awareness? Gratitude *is* an outflow of love. Wondering on this, and still filled with gratitude I rounded a bend. Three deer stood in my path ten yards ahead. At my appearance they glanced up unalarmed and then resumed grazing. I stopped, reluctant to disturb them. I stood a minute, deeply thankful for their friendliness.

I had little time to linger though and rode forward. To my surprise they did not move though I passed by almost within arm's length.

Through this I felt the deer had answered my question. Gratitude could be the presence I sought. I stopped that day before leaving the meadow, turned back and whispered "Thank you" to three deer. Then I left in awe, the way I always leave the woods if I have been clear enough to see what is there.

A Welcome

My noisy tenant was acting up. I was fearing failure, and this fear alternated with an equally strong fear of success. I stayed away from the woods for some time. Then one day I sensed I was missing support there and I returned.

As I entered, fanned out facing me were more deer than I could count at a glance. They were still but not startled. There were full-grown deer and little ones nearly concealed by low foliage. I searched their eyes. I absorbed their gentle spirit and rested in it. "We've been waiting for you," came the message. Then slowly one by one they turned and disappeared in several directions into the woods.

Chipmunk Guidance

Every time a chipmunk darts across my trail, if I am present enough, I gain a lesson. If my mind has wandered, I am called back to attention. If I am focused, I am urged on by their high spirits. One appearance however, served a deeper purpose.

I was biking fast when a chipmunk darted into the trail and stopped dead center, facing me head on. Standing little more than an inch high, it boldly blocked my path.

I braked and stood looking down in breathless wonder. My heart pounded. Surely this had meaning, but what could it be? My mind reeled. I rifled through interpretations but none rang true. The chipmunk and I were deadlocked.

A moment later it moved to the side of the trail and stopped, looking at me as if it knew that waiting was pointless. "You poor thing," it seemed to be saying. "Don't you get it?" I sensed I should move on and pedaled forward bewildered at having been found wanting by a rodent, but I was to be given another chance.

I was barely up to speed when an instant replay occurred. A second chipmunk darted into my trail just as the first had, stopping dead center. Again I was blocked, but this time the message came through loud and clear: "STOP!" How could I have missed it!

I had been told to stop, and stop I did. I stopped riding. I stopped thinking. I stopped looking for guidance and trying to find meaning. Instantly my tiny teacher shot away and vanished in the brush.

I was silent now and empty. A pale green panorama of early spring filled me with beauty. I gazed slowly side-to-side across the tree-scape. My gaze rose slowly upward until I saw the sky through the tree tops.

Dense clouds had been in place for days and were now breaking up. The trees were still but upper level winds filled the sky with motion. Billowing layers, gunmetal gray to white as snow were drifting apart. Edges of clouds concealing the sun caught fire as they separated. The forest's soft glow became vibrant as the sun broke free dazzling my eyes.

I did not look for meaning here. There was no need to. I lived its meaning. It was a run-through of my life's work. I was being told to struggle through the barrier of words and clear away what blocks the truth.

Now the sun owned the sky. Facing its pure light a prayer emerged from the depths of my soul: "May you be free to flow through me."

Then all was silent.

We tend to deny events like those described here. We might dismiss them as "supernatural." If you experience *mystery* however, instead of denial, you open a door to awareness. Pass through and there will be more meaning and purpose to your life than you have perhaps imagined. Let mystery beacon you in.

Our present-day concept of human nature is a narrowly confining conceptual box. We call things "supernatural" when this concept of human nature does not permit them. If we knew human nature through awareness however, events like these might seem quite natural. Our deepest nature is all but unknown to us. Unitarian Minister Nancy Newhall said: "The wilderness holds answers to questions man has not yet learned to ask. "

Awareness of Truth and the End of Suffering

Meditation tradition promises an "end to suffering." It ends when awareness of truth replaces concepts as our locus of control. When blindness ends, needless suffering ends.

Chapter Four showed how we "run concepts" the way computers run programs. When we do, concepts run us. Concepts, not awareness decide our thoughts and actions. When a concept is highly inconsistent with reality we suffer most.

Using some everyday concepts, I want to illustrate how awareness can free us from suffering. First, consider the concept of being alone.

-    Being Alone

My daughter left for college at the same time my husband was working out of state. It was the first time I had ever lived alone. To my surprise, at times of strong awareness I had no problem with being alone. I was not running an "empty nest" program. When fully aware, there was no possibility of being alone.

Thoreau experienced this. He was not a hermit by nature and had many close friends. At first he feared the solitude of Walden Pond, but one day thinking he lacked company he "became conscious of a slight insanity:"

> *In the midst of a gentle rain while these thoughts prevailed, I was suddenly sensible of such sweet and beneficent society in Nature, in the very pattering of the drops, and in every sound and sight around, an infinite and unaccountable friendliness...an atmosphere sustaining me, as made the fancied advantages of human neighborhood insignificant, and I have never thought of them since.*

"How could I possibly feel alone," he wrote. "Is not our planet in the Milky Way?"

The "slight insanity" is our illusion of separation. It is created by thoughts of self. It ends with awareness. Being "alone" is a concept that is inconsistent with reality, another accident of speech. In truth you are not separated from loved ones by distance or even by death. Deepest awareness sees this.

- Deathless

Our concept of death goes hand in hand with the gradual deterioration program. At breakthrough I saw how inconsistent with reality that concept of death is. Awareness frees you from death. A Zen story illustrates how.

The town's people fled the conqueror, but the Zen Master stayed sitting at the temple gate. "Don't you know I can run you through without batting an eye," said the warrior? "Don't you know I can be run through without batting an eye," the Master replied? Death posed no threat.

A present day Zen Master was diagnosed with cancer. When offered treatment options he asked: "Is the cancer a living thing?" "Yes" was the answer. "Let it grow," he said.

Death posed no threat to Gandhi when an assassin stepped from a crowd and shot him. He folded his hands in a gesture of forgiveness, recited his mantra uniting himself with the Divine, and passed on.

Such fearlessness looks like the strength of steel, but it is the softness of no resistance. It comes when awareness frees you from death. I was astonished at breakthrough to see that death is nothing. I saw that there are no "dead people" in the cemetery. "Dead" is not something a person can be.

The concept of death is an illusion that Ram Dass penetrated. He visited an elderly Quaker woman who had been ill for a long time. She said she was not afraid to die but was simply tired of dying. "Couldn't you just die, say...twenty minutes each hour?" he suggested. She had been running a "dying program" and doing some unnecessary suffering.

"Lead me from the unreal to the real," says the Upanishads. "Lead me from death to immortality." Awareness does this. An Indian Swami said he "became conscious of eternal life. I saw that all men are immortal...I knew that what the vision showed me was true. That conviction has never been lost (in Saraswati, 1976, page 46)."

"I know I am deathless," wrote Whitman. "All goes onward and outward, nothing collapses, and to die is different from what anyone supposed and luckier." At the end of life, light is continuous.

At the funeral of a beloved friend, his enlightened companions chanted happily:

Hey, Sung Ho!
Where'd you go?

Hey, Sung Ho!
Where'd you go?
You have gone
Where you really were.
And we are here—
Damn it! We are here (Chuang Tzu, in Merton, 1965, page 55)*!*

Having seen through death I hope to use my power of awareness to catapult myself into where I go next. "If you are free, there is immortality for you, if you are free (Vivekananda, 1987, page 393)."

-    Timeless

Is there something hanging over your head? If so, it hangs there suspended from a cable: your concept of time. If what hangs over you is something good (a vacation, a promotion or enlightenment for instance), you suffer needlessly nevertheless; still missing payday. Eckhart Tolle said much that is useful in understanding this problem.

The concept of time is also a health hazard. Cardiologists see a "hurry sickness" in hypertension. Free of the time concept the pressure is off. The cable breaks, and the specters hanging over you disperse. In place of time-pressure is serene, spacious timelessness:

I hereby leave and bequeath
In perpetuity
To this bird this fence (Issa).

Anne Lindburgh passed someone on the beach and exchanged a smile:

The smile, the act, the relationship is hung in space, in the immediacy and
purity of the present; suspended on the still point of here and now; balanced
there, on a shaft of air, like a seagull (1955, page 64).

Awareness sees that units of time are arbitrary mental constructs. Seeing through time frees you of the concept of "now" too. (Now implies later; the program runs on.) Physicists agree that nothing real answers to the name "time." Reality is always present.

"Time is but the stream I go a-fishing in," wrote Thoreau. "I see the bottom and detect how shallow it is. Its thin current slides away, but eternity remains (page 71)."

-    <u>Ageless</u>

The party was for me and someone said "Happy birthday!" "Happy birthday to you" I answered, as a "Good morning" might be returned. Everyone laughed at the strange mistake, but I was awed by it. For the first time I realized the extent to which I was free of the age concept.

I mentioned the Magic Slate earlier. The marks on your slate are concepts. Aging or "gradual deterioration" is one. Clearing your head cleans your slate. Negative expectations, autosuggestions and self-limiting specifications of the program are wiped away. You get free of "aging" in the same way Ram Dass freed his friend the Quaker woman from "dying." Free of the age concept you are ageless.

I have experienced the difference this freedom makes. A number in response to "how old am I," has little meaning for me. One's ageless essence becomes a living truth. If you stop running the age program you may find that widely varying ages can coexist in you.

A clean slate sets your inner-child free. As the phrase goes, you play again with a child's zeal; listen with a child's wonder; act with a child's innocence and love with a child's heart.

The wisdom that comes with age can develop ahead of chronological years because awareness accelerates growth.

Not running "gradual deterioration" may also slow biological aging by letting your body violate dictates (doing more physically over time, for instance, instead of less). Freedom from subconscious suggestions of debilitation may even impact at the cellular level.

It is possible to be so free of age that chronological age has little or no bearing on your life. Your "age" can be no more than a number in somebody else's head if you do not hold it in yours. Not long ago, when asked my age in a doctor's office I had to do the math.

Awareness may be the closest thing you will find to a fountain of youth. Drink its cool, clear waters. As the sage said: "Renew thyself completely each day. Do it again and again and forever again."

- Selfless

"Self" is a concept. It is mind-made. The illusion of self however, seems utterly real. This is because your concept of yourself is unlike other concepts in one vital respect. Other concepts can be distinguished from things they represent. We easily see that air and the concept of "air" are two different things. (You can not breathe the concept.) But the concept of self fools us because the concept is the *only* self there is. No *real* thing exists to contrast it with. Children are fooled by the "equator" concept in this way. Since the concept is the only equator there is, they assume a line must really encircle the earth. "Self" and "equator" are equally mind-made, equally deceptive, confusing concepts.

When you no longer see your self in it, you are liberated. The self-interest program shuts down and with this comes a feeling of freedom that is beyond words. Imagine feeling so selfless that you have absolutely no idea you are selfless. This is Great Liberation.

Very rarely have I known such awareness, but when I have, I have been a full-grown newborn with no personal history and no constraints from past experience. I have no concept of myself; no thought of myself, no self-consciousness or self-interested action. I am what a human being is when you clear away everything: pure awareness and the love this allows to flow.

Meeting someone selfless is no ordinary meeting. Ordinarily, the first thing we do is size someone up. "What kind of person is this?" Answers come easily since others want us to know who they are. They project personas and we peg people with concepts right away. But when I do not see myself, others can't either. In rare moments when I am fully present there is no *who* upfront, no persona, no mask, not even age or gender programs. Someone trying to judge is at a loss.

Babies are not confused because they know through awareness, not opinion and judgment. They plainly see what is there. Adults trying to peg me find it difficult and masks do not stick (even those I might like to put on myself). Master Deac saw my soul on first meeting but such clarity is as rare as full awareness.

Meeting No-self

As we saw in Chapter Five, love flows only when there is connection. Absence of thoughts of self completes the circuit. If awareness meets awareness there is union. I have encountered people suddenly in store isles and on elevators and without time for judgment they are *caught aware*. No-self meeting no-self is a meeting of hearts. Such meetings are surprising and gratifying.

Some people have been overjoyed at being reunited with me. They are sure they know me and ask where I grew up, where I live. If I denied knowing them they were confused so I stopped denying it. "Yes I do know you," I say. In truth, I do.

Other encounters have been richer still. I passed an elderly man in a grocery isle. His head did not turn from the shelf he faced. I stopped several feet away looking at the shelf. Without looking at me he began talking as if we had been together for hours. His diabetic brother had broken a hip. There were complications with surgery and a poor prognosis. He was describing his own failing health when suddenly he realized he was talking to a complete stranger. He was frightened. I turned and faced him and simply stood there. I had no words of comfort to offer, nothing to say.

A woman in a rest room came up behind me as I washed my hands. Our eyes never met yet she outpoured a family history of sadness, a sister's death, a brother's alcoholism, her husband's arthritis, her son's divorce. She spoke quickly, perhaps sensing that this strange intimacy would soon end. I turned to her and stood in silence. Again I had no words.

I was checking out in a market when a young cashier looked up and told me her father had come home drunk the night before and wet his pants in the bedroom. She said only that. I said nothing.

Another time I stepped on an elevator and pressed a button for my floor. By my side was a woman I had never seen. She began talking before the door closed. She had lost her husband and through his illness she had not been there for him as she might have been.

I felt deeply grateful for such encounters, yet I always felt I was failing people. Now I think my silence is just what they needed. They reached through it into my awareness and found help there. The woman on the elevator needed to forgive herself and used my awareness of what a human being is. Knowing myself, I know I am as bad (and as good) as this woman. To judge or condemn her (or anyone else) would mean throwing myself out too. I had the understanding she needed to forgive herself.

The cashier, the man in the store and the woman in the rest room also used my awareness. To ease their pain they needed acceptance. When I am very clear I know that all things are as they must be and should be. This liberating truth opens a heart of bliss in a world of pain. Entering the larger space of an open heart makes pain smaller.

I worry less now about lacking words. To be of use I need awareness. Words can facilitate awareness however. I use them as "fertilizer" as Master Deac suggests. "I am nothing...Nothing but awareness..." centers me in an open heart. "Mouth shut; heart open...Mouth shut; heart open," reminds me what I am.

Love: The Operating Principle

One final insight came to me at breakthrough. It came unbidden in the afterglow after all my questions had been answered; all "Whys" put permanently to rest. My silence was broken with these words: *Love is the operating principle of the whole thing.*

This was not a welcome insight. "How strange," I thought. "Love... an *'operating principle?'*" This did not appeal to my scientific taste, yet knowing where this came from I did not question it. I simply put the concept aside and left it there for many years.

Now through awareness, and with the certainty of laws governing the physical universe, I know its meaning. What is must be and *should be* because *love* is the basis of the Plan: the operating principle of the whole thing. Everything moves toward this end. Life's pain calls you to awareness and if you answer the call, awareness returns you to selfless action, selfless love.

Selfless Love

We see the operating principle in force in selfless action. Not based on a self-interest agenda it has another locus of control. Selfless acts arise from awareness as effortlessly as plants grow. They are not contrived like good deeds but flow spontaneously like my little one's action when she reached out to heal my foot. Such action comes naturally in full awareness when as Zen puts it, "Using no supernatural power you bring withered trees to bloom."

On rare occasions I experience such selflessness. At these times I am a vibrant center of awareness. I have no plan, no agenda and no idea what is going to happen next. Life is unimpeded outflow, a frictionless glide with no dis-ease, no discord, no social awkwardness, no anxiety. At such times I do not love. Love loves, and actions bring greater joy than anything I could possibly think up to do to be happy.

Some actions arise out of empathy too deep for the thinking mind to access or understand. I have said things that helped others feel better about themselves, without prior knowledge that could have told me what to say. Did I divine it through awareness? Did the Divine intervene, or are these one and the same thing? Christian tradition says that giving up your will you do the "Will of God." The Bible says "Trust in the Lord with all thine heart and lean not upon thine own understanding (Proverbs 3:5)."

Selfless words and actions align with the Plan's direction. We become "aligned with our Creator" as Wayne Dyer put it (2006, page 58). You do not "intend" to do good deeds. Love does not intend. Action flows like water in a current that powers the universe as with infinite grace the Plan unfolds. You take no credit for any good that comes. Taking credit is like a nasty virus you do not want to catch. It is ego strength at the cost of freedom. I find I do not need ego strength if I have real power: if I have love.

- ### Love is Power

For most of my life I lived with a mystery. I knew I would teach a particular lesson. I knew it would be: *love is power.* I knew I would teach this with bottomed-out certainty, yet I had no knowledge of the subject and no interest in it either. I see now that I had to learn the lesson before I could teach it. Not long ago I did.

It was a frigid December day. I drove to a collection depot with a bag of clothes for the needy. The attendant had just returned from lunch. He wore no gloves or hat and an unzipped jacket flapped in the wind. With raw red hands he struggled to cover a CLOSED sign with a black plastic bag.

He did not see me approach so I announced myself. "Open for business," I asked?

He turned in a rage, both arms swinging from six feet away. "You are *so stupid*," he roared. "Can't you see I'm *here*? HOW STUPID ARE YOU!"

At that moment I felt his pain, not his current pain but his whole life's pain. In a moment of pure awareness I read his secret history. I saw through the madman to an innocent child that nothing had ever touched. An insight came: to rage is to writhe in pain. There followed a surge of love.

Drawn to him, I walked closer, my eyes fixed gently on his. "Can I help you," I asked?

With these words I felt a wave of love leave my body, a tangible physical force so strong that nothing could have diverted it. A gale met a candle flame; his rage was extinguished, and when he spoke I heard the voice of another man. "Don't worry about me," he said.

No other words were spoken. None were needed. I gave him my package and left. As I drove away in awe, an insight resounded in me: "*Power*! Love is *power*."

Every Christmas under cover of darkness I leave a small gift marked: "For the Attendant," my thanks to my guide.

Invulnerable

In *Siddhartha* we see love's power to end pain. His suffering ended with acceptance. He stopped comparing his life to some desired imaginary world—"some mind-made vision of perfection." He loved the world and was glad to belong to it. "Everything is good," he said, "death as well as life…wisdom as well as folly. Everything is necessary, everything needs only my agreement, my assent, my loving understanding; then all is well with me and nothing can harm me (Hesse, page 144)." Love's power made him invulnerable.

It has been said that at the moment of enlightenment "a wandering cur frightened by street urchins" becomes "a lion with a golden mane whose roar strikes terror in the hearts of all feeble spirits (in Benoit, *The Supreme Doctrine*, 1955, page 116)." Love and you are this lion. Vulnerability ends.

In true selflessness one can not be intimidated. Love is fearless *because* it is selfless. No self is there to be harmed.

In love no insult is possible. "To be in harmony with the oneness of life," says Buddhism, "is to be without anxiety about imperfection." An insult, like an arrow shot at the sun, evaporates in the pure flame.

You cannot suffer jealousy and envy. Awareness ends separation so everyone's good fortune is your own.

You cannot be angered. Love is too clear sighted for this. You see that anyone threatening you is blind. Who could be angry at a blind man for stumbling in the way? Love flows in response to attack, source to sink, magnetically drawn to hidden perfection, the love at the center. Love is your response to threat because when innocence is seen, there is no other way to relate. Anything but love would be false, and when selfless, nothing false remains.

It is impossible to deceive love. You cannot relate falsely to truth. If you try, with nothing there to come up against you fall into an abyss.

Love's force cannot be opposed since it offers no resistance. Opposing love, you are like a locomotive moving on tracks that suddenly end. You collide with your own force.

Love shields like armor. Not even threat of death can touch love. After all, you are in heaven already. What harm could come?

Love is your power to lift a car off your child. It is the power to throw yourself on a grenade to save your friends. Love is the highest authority; the ultimate design principle; the ultimate force. It is life's meaning and purpose, the whole aim and end of existence. It is your true nature. Conceive of nothing and this heaven is yours.

Living Awareness

Master Deac says awareness is everything. I want to honor his words. I want to live in awareness: to know by means of it, to act out of it, to love because of it.

When Master Choe told his disciple: "You know it is destiny that we meet," the young soldier looked up and recognized truth. He had not looked for guidance. He was not searching for meaning and purpose. He was aware enough that these found him.

Awareness is the facilitator of destiny. When the Chauffeur drives, destiny is being fulfilled. In this state, as Wayne Dyer puts it in his book *Inspiration*, "our purpose will not only find us, it will 'chase after' us wherever we go (2006, page 58)." I saw my destiny at breakthrough. It was to write this book. To that end, in the final phase of writing, destiny took me to Master Deac. Without my knowing it, this course had been set mysteriously long before, at the time of my breakthrough. Let me explain.

At that time the *Kung Fu* TV show was popular. In its flashbacks to the Shaolin Monastery I saw the very same insights I was having through meditation and I became keenly interested in *Kung Fu* philosophy.

Then a *dojo* opened at my street corner. A big KUNG FU sign confronted me every day as I passed by. I was drawn in. I was signing up for lessons and the teacher asked: "Why do you want to learn Karate?" I was dumbfounded. I had no answer. Then the strangest realization occurred. I had not intended to learn Karate. I was there, but being there was *not my plan*.

I sat speechless, but the teacher waited for an answer. "Well," I fumbled, "I like to dance."

This started me off badly and my stay there was not long. I put Karate behind me and gave it no thought for many years. My being there however, was no accident. It had a reason, and only now can I see what that reason was.

Fast-forward to a drizzly winter night two decades later. I was twenty minutes early for an appointment in town. Rather than sit waiting in my car I looked for a place to escape the weather.

Close by was a bright, well-maintained, welcoming sort of building with a Martial Arts sign. My early Kung Fu experience made me feel comfortable walking in, though I had no intention of staying. There I was introduced to Master Deac. He said: "You know it is destiny that we meet," and strangely, I did know. I had sensed it even before he said those words. I stayed; I became a disciple of Master Deac and this is how it came to be that he entrusted to me the words of the tradition. Now I have entrusted them to you. They came to you like a leaf on the water.

Caveat: Truth is not What You Think

Reading these pages, phantoms may have taken life in your imagination. Take warning. Remember that truth is not what you think. It is what you are aware of. Words can not substitute for awareness.

Truth takes life when images fade and false contrivances of words break down. Then "solitude will not be solitude; nor poverty poverty; nor weakness weakness (Thoreau)." You will see that beauty and love are of one nature; love and happiness are not two different things, and awareness and love cannot be separated. So do not seek truth in words or in illusions conjured by poets. Truth is "indescribable, inconceivable, unutterable (Buddha)."

> *Four men out walking came to a place enclosed by a wall. One scaled the wall and looking over said: Ah...ah! and dropped in. A second climbed the wall and looking over said: Ahhhhh, and dropped in. A third did so, and then the fourth. Now who could tell what is inside* (Sri Ramakrishna, 1985, page 38)?

Action, not words brings presence in your mansion. Throw the book aside and see for yourself.

CHAPTER THIRTEEN
HOW TO SEE GOD

Don't Believe. See and Experience.
Brother Lawrence

What you need to know: Running a "religion program" can limit spiritual life. The blindness keeps us from seeing God. Spiritual fulfillment awaits awareness.

As a child I loved to play in a patch of woods near my home. I climbed trees and swung on vines, but the still moments were best. I planted a little carpet of moss at the foot of a maple. On windy days its leaves flickered wildly and sunlight filtering through made a dazzling display on the dark brown earth. I sat alone and watched in ecstasy.

As an adult I found heaven again in my neighbor's wood. Across a small creek at the back of my yard lie ten acres of maples laced with pines. In spring it fills with the fragrance of wildflowers, in winter with deep silent snow. Awareness comes naturally to me there, and with it comes guidance and a deep sense of reverence.

One day however I entered the woods going on in my head about something. I walked for several minutes oblivious to everything. Then something took my breath away. I felt as if something was terribly wrong. I felt I was *ignoring God*.

Buddha called thoughts defilements. "Defile" is the perfect word. When we are busy in our heads we are blind to sacred presence, and we can be blind to this presence even in Church. Our five percent limit on awareness limits spiritual fulfillment to a like extent. It can rule out seeing God.

Christian tradition has shown us the way, but we have lost some of the directions. Here we take a second look. We start with Brother Lawrence's teachings on how to enter "The Presence of God."

Brother Lawrence's Practice of the Presence of God

Hesse said of Siddhartha: "He did not speak but his face silently radiated love and serenity, understanding and knowledge." I imagine Brother Lawrence (1605 to 1691) might have looked like this. Lawrence was a Carmelite Brother. A biographer called him a simple man, frank and open, with no pious air and no show of superiority. Though he never wrote a book his wisdom was apparent, and his words were written down and preserved. They come to us in a small volume: *The Practice of the Presence of God.* Let's look at Brother Lawrence's how-to.

- The How-to

If we asked Lawrence "How do you enter the presence of God?" he might have said: "You don't need to. You are already there."

If we asked: "Why don't we know it?" he would surely have said: "Your thoughts stand in the way."

"Thoughts are of little or no actual use," said Lawrence. "They are not conducive to our salvation, and we should not spend our lives captives of them." We are kept from the best in life said Lawrence, by "trifles and fooleries."

His solution to this problem was simple. "Rivet attention," he said. "Hold yourself before God like a dumb and paralyzed beggar at a rich man's gate. Concentrate! Intensity of concentration will drive from your mind everything that can displace God."

Attention

Attention was Lawrence's method of prayer. He felt "spiritual dryness" in ordinary, spoken prayer. He preferred "simple attention with a loving gaze upon God." He was able through continuous discipline, to practice this *at all times.* Work time in the monastery's busy kitchen was no different from prayer time. "Every hour, every minute" he attended "to small things for the love of God."

When he first began his practice Lawrence often lost attention, sometimes for long periods, but this did not upset him. Instead of blaming himself, he "acknowledged his wretchedness," and then started again, "more confident for having known the sadness of the habitual mind."

Lawrence warns us that distractions are inevitable. Some come by necessity ("Who is at the door?"); others through weakness ("I'd rather be napping."). Stay with it, he promises, and all such impediments can be overcome.

Perseverance

Persevere and over time attention comes easier. Eventually, said Lawrence, deep awareness comes "with great felicity, even taking us by surprise" (as did my moment of sudden clarity with the frog). It comes without trying. At times Lawrence felt his "spirit uplifted without any effort...suspended and held in God as in its center and place of rest." Persist he said, until "the ordinary mind is no more," and awareness is "habitual and natural."

Lawrence was clearly a Monarch of Mind; his true nature manifest. Even working in the noisy confusion of the kitchen at mealtime, Lawrence found "the same peace of soul and tranquility of spirit" as on his "knees at the Blessed Sacrament."

Molinos and "Blessed Silence"

Like Lawrence, Spanish priest Miguel Molinos (1628 to 1696) preferred silence to ordinary payer. His *Spiritual Guide which Disentangles the Soul* (first published 1685) was proclaimed by the Church: "a priceless jewel, and a manual of piety and perfection." The *Guide* became a bestseller, leading multitudes of Christians to a practice called "contemplation."

-   Molinos on "Contemplation"

"It is not through thinking that the soul draws near to God," he wrote. It is through "contemplation." Its aim is silence: "silence of words, silence of desires, and silence of thoughts." Molinos called "the first perfect, the second more perfect, and the third most perfect."

Remain calm and silent, he wrote. The rewards of this practice will far surpass those of spoken prayer:

Prayer sows and Contemplation reaps.
Prayer seeks and Contemplation finds.
Prayer prepares the Food. Contemplation savors it and feeds on it.

A Mind Controlled and Subdued

"A mind controlled and subdued" is the objective of contemplation practice. "Undisciplined minds are always in bad habits of wandering and dissipation. Free yourself of imagination, emotion and reasoning," said Molinos, and your soul will "come to herself again:"

uplifted into a passive state, quiet, void and peaceful,...quiet of fears; void of affections, desires, and thoughts, and peaceful in temptations and tribulations.

Empty yourself thus and you become a filled container. Disentangled souls have "communion" with God. This is not a relationship but union with sacred presence. It is not the "visions and raptures some might expect," said Molinos. "Experience that is ecstatic and exalting will pass and be gone." In contemplation, you never lose command of "sense and reason." You stay "lovingly aware."

Master Choe called union with nature "prayer." Awareness of this depth sees "divinity in a leaf of grass...and heaven in a wildflower." Edna Millay had a like experience: "God, I can push the grass apart and lay my finger on Thy heart!" At times like this we do not *believe* in God. We *see and experience*. Now let's look at the elements of practice.

Elements of Practice: Attention and Perseverance

For Lawrence and Molinos, the key elements of practice are attention and perseverance.

- Attention

Father Thomas Keating says "clear away mental clutter and reach: a still point, connecting directly with infinite love (*Intimacy With God*, 1996)." This clearing derives from attention, the basic practice of Lawrence and Molinos.

The rule of simplicity applies here. Attention is both necessary and sufficient for success. You need nothing more, and nothing more can be added without taking away from your practice. You simply yield the right of way to the Chauffeur. Lawrence and Molinos never say, for instance: "Try to enter the presence of God." This would be bondage to an idea. Seeking God interferes with seeing God.

Eastern tradition says that believing "God is there" is ignorance. Awareness that "God is here" is knowledge. The presence is gained through seeing, not seeking God.

Nor need you try to "surrender." This would be an act of will. *Active* surrender is not necessary. What you need, in signal to noise terms, is signal with a capital "S." Then the barrier falls away like a hatchling's shell and you see the light:

> *for that which illumines the Soul is that which it is to see, just as it is by the sun's own light that we see the sun.*
> *How is this to be accomplished?*
> *Cut away everything* (Plotinus, in Harvey, 1996, page 135).

Sharp attention, your pruning shears, is all your practice requires, but you must persevere.

• Perseverance

You have to stick to it, and obstacles to this do arise. One is the *appearance* of the exercise. "Onlookers will accuse you of inactivity," said Molinos, "but though it seems that thou dost nothing...the advantage is infinite." Lawrence warned that its appearance might give you "a haunting suspicion that the effort is a waste of time." This is illusion. "You must go on," he tells us, "making up your mind to persevere until death, whatever the difficulties may be."

Perseverance in attention means you "pray always" as the Bible says (Luke 21). St. Augustine said: "True, whole prayer is nothing but love." Awareness born of attention permits continuous outflow.

Molinos too called for full time effort. "This ought to be thy chief and continual exercise (page 186)," he said. And if you see no progress, stick to it just the same. Lawrence promises eventual breakthrough. "Knock at the door and keep on knocking," he said. "It will open and you will be given, all of a sudden what you have awaited so long."

They agree that mind resists control and attention comes hard, especially at first. With great determination however, progress may be faster than you might guess. Molinos said highest goals can be reached in "two to six months, but should it take longer: as its formation is difficult, so will your joy be great when it is attained (page 77)." He adds that if full time effort is not possible, devote part time. (As in attention focusing practice, you must quiet the mind periodically but efficiently.) Molinos said that even brief periods of silence "will bring more favor than the soul could ever have hoped for." And what is this favor? According to Lawrence it is "the standard by which all happiness should be judged."

Happiness: The Reward of Practice

"Happiness" is the reward of practice. Used here however, the word intends more than we mean by it in everyday use. It means the full gratification of presence in your mansion. As noted before, Lawrence called full awareness an "all-sufficing state."

- True Happiness: The All-sufficing State

When love is real you feel you can live on love alone. This is the all-sufficing state I saw in my little one. Having things had nothing to do with her happiness and lack of things did not destroy it. Separated from nothing, she lacked nothing. Nothing was not hers. She had "nirvana," extinction of needs. There is no need for *self*-gratification when no needy self exists.

A monkey reaches in a bottle and grabs an apple. As long as he holds it he is stuck. To see yourself in it is to get stuck like this, stuck going the wrong way in pursuit of happiness. Letting go however, full gratification comes automatically.

Spiritual traditions understand the problem of self-interest. "Aim for true and perfect annihilation" of will, said Molinos. As noted in Chapter Five, Eastern tradition sees a like solution. "What may I do that Divine Love may be reflected in my heart," asks the student? "Annihilate the desire-self!" is the answer (Vaswani, undated). "Put out self," says another sage, "lose it, forget it: just let God work. The less self, the more God comes in (Vivekananda, 1987, page 393)." Free of self-interest, the Chauffeur takes the wheel. Your life aligns with the direction of the Plan (consistent with reality), not seeking guidance, but carried effortlessly the right way.

Progress in Karate dō involves elimination of self. Master Deac designed The Martial Arts Center teaching area such that students only are permitted. Spectators would make students self-conscious. A clean, quiet, orderly environment engenders a like mind-state. *Katas* are moving meditations, precision movements practiced with the aim of "purity and perfection." Master Deac calls this practice a powerful cleansing that brings permanent change.

C. S. Lewis said he prayed, not to change God but to change himself. Blessed silence changes you. Wanting something for yourself, the cause of unhappiness, is eliminated in the process. Spontaneous, effortless right action follows. "Mind, purged of its dust and dirt...becomes pure and holy (Narayananda, page 78)." Then no barrier to love's outflow exists, and freedom from suffering follows naturally.

Freedom from Suffering

"A soul in this state," said Lawrence, "is incapable of misery." Invulnerability: immunity to suffering comes with the all-sufficing state. Brother Lawrence saw love as healing waters behind a dam. To Molinos love is "a Refuge where no harm or injury can come." He saw love's power as "a Fortress which defends, protects and fights for thee." Eastern tradition calls love: "an impregnable tower...which no danger can disturb (in Merton, 1965, page 134)." At the same time it "feels so tranquil" that in it Lawrence feared nothing. He felt so "secure and gratified, that like a babe in its mother's arms," he could "willingly dare call it the breasts of God."

-   The Feel of Communion

Full awareness brings the union or Communion of Christian tradition. Formerly you were noise: "a resounding gong or a clanging cymbal." With silence comes union. In Hinduism such happiness is referred to as "Bliss and Peace Unchanging."

Lawrence described the state as "beauteous, peaceful, unearthly, reverent, humble, loving, and very simple." "Joys indescribable" come with it, "joys so great that the least turning away is a hell."

Playwright Eugene O'Neil captured the feel of union. A man lay on a ship's deck, masts with moonlit sails towering above him:

For a moment I lost myself—I was set free! I dissolved into the sea, became white sails and flying spray, became beauty and rhythm, became moonlight and the ship and the high dim-starred sky! I belonged, without past or future, within peace and unity and a wild joy, within something greater than my own life, or the life of Man...To God, if you want to put it that way (Long Day's Journey Into Night).

Missing the union awareness creates is missing ultimate reality, missing love. Hinduism calls ultimate reality "a condition where one is in supreme bliss (in Elliott, 1995, page 226)."

> *It is the most exalted state...the highest bliss a being can enjoy. This is the greatest attainment and when compared with it even the acquirement of a mighty empire is nothing...After attaining this state once the man becomes Free. He is not bound by anything. He sees the Divine Hand in everything. He moves freely with full peace and without the least worry...his mind is ever fixed in the Supreme Reality* (Narayananda, page 78).

And what is "Supreme Reality?" It is what is *here now*. As Rachael Remen said: "The sacred lives beyond labels and judgment (1996, page 71)." To be fully aware anywhere feels like adoring God. Any place you are aware will be sacred to you. The sacred is "above us, beneath us, beside us, within us, what need have we for temples made with hands (Newell, 1997, page 86)?"

Just raise your eyes and look about and you will be radiant at what you see. "Heaven is where you are, and when you can see heaven, you can see it even in hell (Satchidananda, in Elliott, 1995, page 228)." In the light of awareness, what is is, must be, and should be, and what is not is not, must not be and should not be. You see the "must be" when awareness penetrates a breathtaking intricacy of all-encompassing inter-relationships in lawful balance. You know why things should be when you find love at the basis of everything, powering the universe, the operating principle of the whole thing. As awareness broadens, the world rights itself. "A view as vast as the sky" sees that heaven is where you are. It sees perfection.

Human Perfection

Master Choe was not pleased with his disciple's move. He had corrected this error often before. Thinking it a small thing, Deac complained: "How many times will I be corrected for this?" "One-thousand times!" affirmed Choe. Master Deac received as much as eleven hours of instruction daily for seven years, his movements endlessly refined. While stationed at Fort Lewis, the two walked in the frigid sand of Puget Sound, Master Choe scrutinizing impressions made by his disciple's feet. Ball had to set before heel. Toes must not turn upward. Blade had to wedge from a certain angle down to a precise depth. Here too, the aim was perfection. There was no compromise. Master Deac holds the same standard. Every minute of a lesson is spent on this discipline. If he interrupts to tell a story, you know you will derive a lesson.

Karate dō with its Buddhist roots, is influenced by the standard of perfection in the Eightfold Path: Perfect Understanding; Perfect Thought; Perfect Speech; Perfect Action; Perfect Work; Perfect Effort; Perfect Mindfulness and Perfect Concentration. The Bible too has a standard of perfection: Corinthians (13:4-8) says of love: "when perfect comes, the imperfect disappears." "Mark the perfect man," reads the Psalm, "for the end of that man is peace (Psalm 37:37)." "Be ye therefore perfect," says Matthew, "even as our Father which art in Heaven is perfect (5:38-48)." Lawrence said: "All may become perfect to the extent that they persevere."

Today however, we rarely hear the word "human" paired with "perfection." If anything, we are discouraged from striving for it. Something changed in the course of history that led us to lower aspirations. We got lost along the way. Let us pause here to consider how this happened.

How We Got Lost

"If thine eye be single," said Jesus, "thy whole body will be filled with light." Attention practice has roots so deep in Christianity that we might well wonder how we got lost. How did we lose the *Spiritual Guide* and its wonderful light? The answer lies in history.

The *Guide* appeared in the age of the Inquisition. The Church at that time scrutinized writings for heresy. As observed before, The *Guide* had been warmly embraced by the Church. The Pope may have seen useful reform in Molinos' teachings and gave him lodgings at the Vatican. Molinos' *Guide* was a blockbuster that went through twenty editions in French, Latin, Italian and Spanish translations in its first six years.

A biographer notes that the Jesuit Order was more alarmed than pleased by this. People were taking spiritual growth into their own hands, bringing into question the need for Clergy. The new movement was so forceful it seemed it might engulf the Church completely. They worried too that since the Pope sanctioned it, he might be cultivating an anti-Jesuit posture.

The Jesuits accused Molinos of heresy and brought the *Guide* for a second time before the judges of the Inquisition. Again the *Guide* was proclaimed in accord with the faith of the Church. Finally they brought political pressure to bear. In a letter to King Louis XIV, the Archbishop of Naples complained of seeing "signs everywhere of a new belief." He claimed to have personally witnessed scores of Christians "sitting as if they were dumb and dead," which offered the Archbishop great trouble and offense. The King, forced to take a stance, complained to the Pope that favor was being shown to "Molinos the heretic."

This turned the tide. Molinos was summoned before the Inquisition and imprisoned. Since many believed his practice the highest expression of the soul, uproar ensued. Molinos was held until the excitement died away. Then the final judgment came. A decree proclaimed the *Guide* "heretical, blasphemous, offensive to pious ears, insolent, dangerous to, and destructive of Christian morality." Molinos was forced to confess to heresy and condemned to prison for life. He survived imprisonment with dignity for ten years. The circumstances of his death are shrouded in mystery.

Ironically, a simple practice of clearing one's head came to be known as an "extreme form of mysticism." To support Molinos was perilous. A woman who corresponded with him and wrote on Blessed Silence was also imprisoned. Anyone who failed to burn Molinos' prayers or writings was subject to excommunication.

These measures brought an end for the most part to such teachings in the Catholic Church. They wiped out Molinos' legacy almost completely. Today however there is new interest in awareness-restoring prayer. I came across a book by a Jesuit priest Father Anthony de Mello, published in 1984 with the Church's formal seal of approval. It begins:

The sooner prayer gets away from thinking the more profitable it becomes. Most priests and religious equate prayer with thinking. This is their downfall (Sadhana, A Way To God: Christian Exercises In Eastern Form. 1984, page 7).

Today you can learn about Molinos *Spiritual Guide* and read Lawrence's letters on the World Wide Web. You can find inspiration here and follow their suggestions, but take care not to go off course. Remember the goal is awareness. To be sure you are on target, stop and confirm attention with feedback.

Real Spirituality

After my father's sudden death I looked to religion for answers. The kind nuns at my Catholic high school gave me a job cleaning the chapel to ease tuition. Undisturbed in that peaceful place I longed for something I could not define. When my work was done I knelt and prayed. Now and then I seemed to touch something beyond myself, but even as this happened I knew it was a flight of imagination. God was not *real* for me.

I had no faith then. Now I know why. It was because I could not see what was before my eyes. In prayer I was lost in the maze, wandering the corridors of mind. I was trapped in a "God" concept, running a "religion program." My concept of God was all I could see.

Rachael Remen called religion "a bridge to the spiritual where most aspirants stay on the bridge (1988)." The bridge is made of concepts that share a noble origin: the truth deep awareness penetrates. Sages went there, saw this truth and came back and spoke of it. We mistook their words for reality and ended up worshiping God the concept.

Dr. Remen reads a moving prayer:

Days pass and the years vanish and we walk sightless among miracles. Lord, fill our eyes with seeing...Let there be moments when your presence like lightening illumines the darkness in which we walk...and we will exclaim in wonder: How filled with awe was this place and we did not know it (Remen, 2001).

This prayer cries out from the bridge, cognizant of hidden fortune. You find that fortune with awareness. "The Kingdom of God is not in word, but in power (1 Corinthians 4:20)." The power is love.

When we set ourselves up in relationship to God, prayer is confined to the dead dry life of words. This separate-self relationship also sustains the self-interest agenda. "Please God, do it my way," prevents outflow of love. "Dear God do it your way," goes with the Plan and this prayer would surely be answered, but then words would not be needed. Love alone would serve.

Love is union, prayer's highest reward. Stop chewing the Divine food, said Molinos, and digest it. Remember:

Prayer sows and Contemplation reaps.
Prayer seeks and Contemplation finds.
Prayer prepares the Food. Contemplation savors and feeds on it.

"The letter killeth," as the Bible says, "but the spirit giveth life (Corinthians 2:3). " We can stop asking to be fed and feast at the banquet. We can fill our own eyes with seeing. We can enter the core of truth and see what the sages saw. When we do, a forest becomes a Cathedral where we dissolve into the sacred and know the place, and ourselves, for the first time. When night falls we see no constellations in the sky. We see our mirrored soul, and all it takes is awareness.

Faith is Awareness of Truth

The battle raged. Choe and his disciple were stuck between opposing forces under heavy artillery fire. Steel-jacketed bullets were flying; noise was deafening and death immanent. The young soldier, agitated, fearful, angry, saw the Master relaxing with his eyes closed. "We could die any second!" he shouted over the din. Master Choe was thoughtful. Then he hollered back:

"Do you believe in God?"

"Yes," yelled the soldier, surprised.

"Do you believe there is something better than this after you die?"

"Of course!" Deac yelled back.

"And your military training, has it prepared you for this battle?"

"My training is the best in the world," the soldier hollered.

"Then which is it you lack faith in," asked Master Choe, "your God or yourself?"

Nothing undermined Choe's faith because it came from awareness. **Awareness of** truth gave him a big picture in any circumstance. He had the perspective that shows that all is as it must be and should be; a God's eye view; a view so vast that light replaces darkness, hope despair. He lived "God realization" as Wayne Dyer calls it. Amidst horrors of war he saw that:

All shall be well, and all shall be well, and all manner of thing shall be well.

Seeing heaven even in hell, he transformed their painful circumstance into a gift of awareness, of wisdom, of love. Master Choe had no dark night.

No Dark Night

Seekers describe a "dark night of the soul," a painful wait for guidance. When you can see what is before your eyes, the waiting ends. Awareness offers continuous guidance. It lights the way so clearly that a dark night is itself illumination: "Open your eyes wider still," it says. Guidance is intrinsic to reality, to life's purpose. "Do not be confused," said Choe. "It surrounds you. It will become part of you." Full awareness sees that nothing in the world ever goes wrong. This knowledge yields perfect faith.

I recall a moment of such faith. I have a strong family history of sudden death. I was going for a stress test and my little girl was worried. I held out my hand, pointed to the center of my palm and said: "If this is the hand of God, I'm right here." I did not mean I would be found healthy. I did not even mean I would survive the stress test. I meant that whatever is must be and should be.

Dr. Wayne Dyer experienced such faith. From the depths of his awareness came the words: "You are not alone. You can count on Me to guide you—and whatever you do, do not doubt My presence (2006, page 245)." "The greatest thing is doubt" only when you are blind to the reality before your eyes.

Some can say: "It was the will of God" and be at peace no matter what. Such faith is *awareness of truth*. I know that at any given time my distance from faith shows how lost I am: how far I am from full awareness.

"Don't believe," said Lawrence. "See and experience." See what is before your eyes. Beliefs are thoughts, and thinking is very far from knowing. The saying "God cannot be represented in words," shows our confusion. *Nothing* can be represented in words without defaulting to concepts, to thinking instead of knowing. God is a metaphor. Awareness sees what the metaphor represents.

When aware we have no "relationship" with God. There is no illusion of separation, no such accident of speech. Instead we are open windows for light to shine through. A Christian mystic said: "Loving is not enough.

We must, like God, ourselves be love (in Harvey, 1996, page 108)." We can be beauty; be truth; be love. Then we will love indiscriminately the way a two-year old does. Looking in someone's eyes we will feel the ecstasy of exquisite beauty without an object as love outflows, drawn magnetically to the love in the other person. This is love so great it feels like we are adoring God, and we are. The "image and likeness" is seen in our eyes.

The fighting Shaolin monks are taught: "Find the spiritual among all the worldly. It will open your mind." Awareness sees that all the worldly is in essence spiritual. Life's meaning and purpose is spiritual. The spiritual is the bottom line.

Now you have the means. You can empty yourself and be filled. You can take delivery on your letters from God and have your spirit uplifted without any effort. Your eyes can see the Divine Hand in everything. Experience ultimate reality and you will see that even to speak is a sacrilege.

One bright autumn day I was at the kitchen table paring apples. My daughter about three then, chattered and played with a little friend on the floor close by me. I was pulling in the reins on mind that day, focusing on the rhythmic paring and on the feel of the glistening fruit. Suddenly I saw things differently. I saw the children but it was no longer "my daughter the three-year-old" and "Reggie her playmate." It was pure, boundless, wordless knowing: the fullness of awareness. It could not be distinguished from love.

Love is our lifeline. Thinking breaks the connection. So take William Henry Channing's advice: "Listen to the stars and birds, to babes and sages with an open heart. Let the spiritual, unbidden and unconscious, grow up through the common." Find Great Love at your kitchen table. As a Zen Master said: "Throw false spirituality away like a pair of old shoes!"

CHAPTER FOURTEEN
BEING LOVE

The brilliant gem is in your hand.
Zen Teaching

W hat you need to know: Happiness does not come from "having it all." It comes from being what you are, from being love. All it takes is awareness.

This book began with Master Choe's words: "We are containers but we have no idea how large we are and we are nowhere near full." In this final chapter we see what a filled container looks like. I chanced on a good description:

> *He literally overflows. He has a treasure of inexpressible joy…and this joy overflows and spreads all around him, filling his surroundings with its fragrance. Light shines from his being. And whether he speaks or is silent, whether he sleeps or is awake, whether he is present or absent, it is always the same thing that he is, the same grace and the same power. His presence or the memory of him conveys something other, something uncreated, tranquil, penetrating…He does nothing which is false. He does not speak, he acts. He does not comment, he simply loves…He has gone out of the realm of our habitual reactions. If you strike him, your blows will not reach him; he is beyond them. If you seek him, wherever you are, you will find him beside you. He lives only for you* (in *Speaking of Silence*, Susan Walker editor, 1987, page 58).

I want to try to bring these words to life for you. They came to life for me through two brief encounters with "filled containers." The first was at a psychology conference in Milwaukee.

I had given a lecture that morning, a comical critique of meditation, exposing flaws in meditation techniques. In my audience were a few hundred clinicians, some clergy, and unknown to me, *a lion with a golden mane.*

Several people came up to greet me afterward. When they left one man took me by surprise, appearing out of nowhere from behind. He was tall and slender, an American, probably in his forties with graying hair. I had never seen a Zen priest and did not recognize the gray robe he wore. Something else was unfamiliar too: though he stood still he seemed somehow animated. I had never seen anyone so much...*there.*

I extended my hand. He took the whole arm and drew me close. He held tightly but his aura held me stronger still. I was spell bound by a shower of light from his eyes.

- Light shines from his being. -

In a whisper and with uncommon kindness he said: "I'm a Zen priest." He said nothing more, but a mental transmission followed like a laser printout in my brain. It told me he welcomed all I had said and that my jokes had not offended.

All throughout this I remained entranced by the light from his eyes, and he remained intent, not loving, but *being love.* His love was a steady-state rapture with no atom of self-consciousness to block its free expression.

The question of "who" he was did not enter my mind. Nothing else did either. I was fully absorbed in what he was, suspended in supreme bliss in the middle of a workday, and this went on and on and on undiminished.

Then suddenly I noticed a woman nearby staring in awe, her mouth gaping. Glancing around I saw others in the same state, frozen to the scene. I became acutely self-conscious and broke away with a fierce jolt. I stood stunned and speechless.

For a moment the priest stood too, studying my predicament. He must have seen that words now would be absurdities, and he left quickly, silently, robe streaming, still radiant, mouth wide open in amazement.

The love I experienced had a long-term effect. It took days just to settle back to earth, and for weeks afterward I benefited. I was less self-critical, lighter, more open and free. I tried to trace the Priest but lacking his name I could not. Since then however, in trying times I have sensed he was with me, supporting me.

- If you seek him, wherever you are, you will find him beside you. -

(If by some happy circumstance he should read this, I thank him for the after care.)

Years later I encountered another such person. I had heard that a Zen Master resided at Springwater, a retreat center a few hours from my home in Western New York. I was told the Master's name was Toni Packer. I assumed the spelling was "Tony" however, and I expected a man.

Curious to see the Master, I drove to Springwater one summer day. I turned in at the entrance, a long curved road through dense woods. Rounding a bend I came on a clearing, or so it seemed from sudden brightness. Strangely though, the trees were as dense. It was not a clearing but merely brightness, and centered in it was a white-haired woman with a smile...How can I put it...a smile that extended beyond her face. It went beyond her face the way the sun's radiance goes beyond the sun. It was palpable in the air, and the trees and leaves partook of it.

- A treasure of joy spreads all around, filling his surroundings...-

She was walking in the woods on a pleasant day, only that, yet such happiness! I expected a "Tony," but I knew instantly this was the Master. The brilliant gem was in her hand.

-    A World of Awareness?

What if the world were filled with such people? What sort of world would an aware world be?

A short story by Dostoevsky (*A Strange Man's Dream*) might give us a glimpse of such a world.

The story begins in the chill of a dreary night. A solitary man, weary of senseless labors, trudges homeward through the rain. A small child appears, soaked through, with tattered, rain-drenched shoes. She calls for help in a voice of despair, something about her mother. She runs to the man and tugs at his elbow. "Call the police for help," he shouts moving on.

Reaching his apartment he is sick from the world's cruelty and from his own. He is certain nothing matters. He loads a gun, intending to end his life. Then in his armchair he falls asleep and dreams.

He dreamt that he used the gun, shot himself, and in death was "conveyed by a guide to a distant star shining in the darkness of space with an emerald sheen." He saw it was another earth. Its flora and fauna, land and sea were exactly the same as our earth's, but now he saw through clear eyes and everything was different. In the union that is awareness, he saw through eyes of love.

There was a wondrous atmosphere. "Everywhere, there was the glow of some festival: a celebration of some great holy final triumph." What Thoreau found in the woods: "an infinite and unaccountable friendliness," that same atmosphere filled this earth.

"A gentle emerald sea softly splashed the shores…and kissed them with an evident, almost conscious love…Tall trees stood in their splendor. Their innumerable leaves greeted him with a soft gentle sound that seemed to speak words of love." Life's fullness, something he had never known, overwhelmed him.

The people of this happy earth gathered round him. A childlike joy was in their faces. They had "the beauty seen in children in their earliest years." A "serene consciousness" was evident too, and their faces were bright with intelligence.

The dreamer knew them at a glance, and at a glance they knew him. They did not need to question him. Their understanding went beyond the limitations of words. They understood everything just by looking in his eyes.

- He does not speak…He does not comment, he simply loves. -

Love flowed from their hearts to heal his pain, love's direction true. With the reliability of mathematical proof, love intervenes. Relieving suffering was their greatest happiness and they "longed to remove every trace of suffering from his face" as soon as possible.

- He lives only for you. -

They did not see themselves in it. They were not self-absorbed but absorbed in reality. They wore no masks. Nothing interfered with being genuinely human.

- He does nothing which is false. -

He knew they were vastly superior to him and wondered how they managed never to offend him or to arouse in him jealousy or envy. It was so because they looked up, not down at him. They could not offend him, and they were self-less so he could not offend them.

- If you strike him, your blows will not reach him; he is beyond them. -

We expect science to give us wisdom and teach us how to live. These people had no such blindness. As in Goethe's poetic phrase: "The inner light shone forth from them so they needed no other light." Their way was lighted by "that which illumines the soul." They sought no "paths" and ran no programs. Love, not words, moved them.

They had no concept of honor or righteousness and no idea of shame. They needed no laws, no commandments or principles to base their lives on. Nor were they confused in thinking "knowledge is superior to feeling; consciousness of life superior to life." Knowing through awareness, their knowledge was "higher and deeper" than knowledge we derive from science.

The dreamer could not understand their knowledge. It was inaccessible to his thinking mind, but "his heart unwittingly absorbed it more and more." In their presence he felt his heart become as innocent and righteous as theirs and he silently worshipped them.

With them he wandered their forests and groves. They pointed out their trees to him and he saw their immense love for the trees. They talked to them "as if talking with beings like themselves." They approached all nature with such intimacy, "communing with stars in the heavens, not only in thought, but in some actual, living way." They had a "constant, uninterrupted, and living union with the totality of the universe."

- His presence conveys something uncreated, tranquil, penetrating…-

When *Siddhartha's* "fearful and proud Self" was gone, he was "like a child, full of happiness and without fear (page 99)." These people were childlike in this way, "playful and high-spirited" with the happiness that comes free. "They rejoiced in their newborns as new sharers of their bliss. Their children were the children of them all, for they were one family."

There were no quarrels or conflicts among them. They were at peace with themselves and each other.

They lived simply, "on the fruits of the trees, the honey from their woods, and the milk of the animals that loved them (page 313)." They were as we are born, with no needs beyond necessities and no cause for worry. They lived as Lindburgh's words suggest: "like a child or a saint in the immediacy of the here and now...every act an island, washed by time and space (1955, page 42)." There was no need to hurry.

Life gratified fully. They did not crave possessions. Possessions would have compromised their freedom and would have added nothing to their happiness, so their work was light. They "rejoiced each night with praise and thanks for the day in melodious songs that flowed from the heart." Their songs were always spontaneous compositions.

- He has gone out of the realm of habitual reactions. -

There was scarcely any illness among them. Their old "died peacefully as though falling asleep, surrounded by those who took leave of them, blessing them, smiling and themselves receiving with bright smiles the farewell wishes of their friends." He saw "no grief or tears" on those occasions but "love that seemed to reach the point of rapture." Being love...

-...it is always the same thing that he is, the same grace and the same power. -

They were deathless. Their earthly union was not cut short by death. "They had knowledge that when earthly joy had reached the limits imposed on it by nature, they would reach a state of still closer communion with the Universe at large. They looked forward to the greater union. They looked forward to the moment with joy."

- **Awakening**

When the dreamer awoke, "boundless rapture uplifted his whole being." He was reborn to "a new, great, powerful, regenerated life." He knew what he had to do now. He would preach hope through words and deeds, and he would seek out that little girl.

He knew that words could not express the truth he had found. He knew he would be mocked for speaking, but he would preach nonetheless. And he did preach, and he was mocked. People called him "a strange man, a ridiculous man." They said it was just a dream, but this did not trouble him. "What is a dream," he mused? "Is life not a dream?" What mattered was that truth in all its glory had been proclaimed to him. Truth was the basis of his vision, "and its living image would fill his soul, set him right and direct his course forever."

- Returning

I remember the day in high school when our Christmas baskets were refused. We returned to school a somber group, perhaps a dozen gifts had been turned away. One student however was excited to see them. She had been graciously welcomed into a home and was eager to go back.

She led a three car caravan through the old part of the city to a wooden house with sagging porch steps. A young couple lived there with their baby and the woman's elderly parents. The young man, their sole support, had been unemployed for a year.

We carried our gifts from our cars as before but something was different now. I felt it as we climbed the steps and entered the kitchen. We were humble enough to give now, and these people were humble enough to receive. Unlike before, there were no haves or have-nots present. We were non-takers all. Givers received and receivers gave and you could not have known which was which. We stood a long while in silence sharing the riches. The kitchen with its old furnishings was luminous, and the baby, too young to understand, understood perfectly and its eyes shone.

You do not have to travel to find your mansion. You do not need to buy anything or join a group or shave your head or read a book. You already have what it takes. Awareness is all you need.

The Ultimate Test

Now take the ultimate self-test. A blade in a clump of grass is the perfect essence of grass. A tree with leaves rustling in the breeze is tree-hood in perfection. Right now be human. Be perfectly human right now.

If you hesitate you do not know what you are.

Find yourself in the silence that waits unmoving, infinitely patient. Do not try to understand it. *Be it* and understanding is complete. Be it and know what you are.

BIBLIOGRAPHY

Sri Aurobindo, *The Adventure of Consciousness*. Pondicherry, India: Sri Aurobindo Ashram Press, 1991.

Aoyama, Shundo, *Zen Seeds, Reflections of a Female Priest*. Tokyo: Kosei Publishing Co., 1990.

Beilenson, Peter (Trans.), *A Little Treasury of Haiku*. New York: Avenel Books, 1980.

Benoit, Hubert, *The Supreme Doctrine*. New York: Inner Traditions International, 1955.

Benson, Herbert, *The Relaxation Response*. New York: William Morrow, 1975.

Chadwick, David, *Thank You and OK: An American Zen Failure In Japan*. New York: Penguin, 1994.

Chandler, Steve, *One Hundred Ways to Motivate Yourself*, N.J.: Career Press, 2004.

Cleary, Thomas (Trans.), *The Original Face: An Anthology of Rinzai Zen*. New York: Grove Press, 1978.

-    Rational Zen: *The Mind of Dogen Zenji*. Boston: Shambhala Publications, 1992.

Connections, January, 1999, #5, Institute of Noetic Sciences, page 26.

Dass, Ram, *Grist for the Mill*. New York: Bantam Books, 1977.

- *Journey of Awakening.* New York: Bantam Books, 1978.

De Mello, Anthony, *The Song of the Bird.* New York: Image Books, 1982.

- *Sadhana, A Way To God: Christian Exercises In Eastern Form.* New York: Image Books, 1984.

Doniger, W. (Trans.), *The Laws of Manu.* London: Penguin Classics 1991, page 117.

Dostoevsky, F., "The Dream of a Ridiculous Man," *The Best Short Stories of Fyodor Dostoevsky.* New York: Modern Library, 2001.

Dyer, Wayne, *Inspiration.* Carlsbad, California: Hay House, 2006.

Eisenberg, David, *Encounters with Qi.* New York: Penguin Books, 1987.

Elliott, William, *Tying Rocks To Clouds.* Wheaton, Illinois: Quest Books, 1995.

Fromm, Erich, *The Art of Loving.* New York: Harper, 1956.

Gallwey, W. Timothy, *The Inner Game of Tennis.* New York: Random House, 1974.

Graham, D. T., Stern, I. A., Winokur, G., The Concept of a Different Set of Physiological Changes in Each Emotion. *Psychiatric Research Reports*, 1960, 12, pages 8-15.

Graham, D. T., Kabler, J. D., Graham, F. K., Physiological Response to the Suggestion of Attitudes Specific for Hives and Hypertension. *Psychosomatic Medicine*, 1962, 24, 159-169.

Greenfield, N. S., Sternbach, R. A., *Handbook of Psychophysiology.* New York: Holt, Rinehart and Winston, 1972.

Hart, William, *The Art of Living: Vipassana Meditation*. New York: Harper Collins, 1987.

Harvey, Andrew (Editor), *Mystics: The Soul's Journey into Truth*. San Francisco: Harper Collins, 1996.

Hesse, Hermann, *Siddhartha*. New York: Bantam Books, 1951.

Herrigel, Eugene, *Zen in the Art of Archery*. New York: Pantheon Books, 1953.

Hyams, Joe, *Zen in the Martial Arts*. New York: Bantam Books, 1982.

Kabat-Zinn, Jon, *Wherever You Go, There You Are*. New York: Hyperion, 1994.

-   *Coming to Our Senses*. New York: Hyperion, 2005.

Kapleau, Philip, *The Three Pillars of Zen*. Boston: Beacon Press, 1965.

Keating, Thomas, *Intimacy with God*. New York: Crossroad Publishing, 1996.

Kei Hua, Ellen, *Kung Fu Meditations and Chinese Proverbial Wisdom*. Ventura California: Thor Publishing Co., 1973.

Kelly, Jack & Marcia, *Sanctuaries: The Complete United States*. New York: Bell Tower, 1996.

Keroauc, Jack, *Some of the Dharma*. New York: Viking, 1997.

Khalsa, S., Stauth, C., *Meditation as Medicine*. New York: Pocket Books, 2002.

Lao Tzu, *The Way of Life*. New York: New American Library, 1955.

Lawrence, Brother, *Practice of the Presence of God*, Donald Attwater (Trans.), Allahabad, India: St. Paul Press, 1981.

Lenz, Frederick, *Surfing the Himalayas.* New York: St. Martin's Press, 1995.

Lindburgh, Anne Morrow, *Gift from the Sea.* New York: Pantheon, 1955.

McMahon, C. E., *Where Medicine Fails.* New York: Trado-Medic Books, 1986.

- Psychosomatic Disease and the Problem of Causation. *Medical Hypotheses*, 2, 112-115,1976.

McMahon, C. E., Parikh, R., *The Sanity Quotient—'SQ' Test.* New York: 1988.

Mehta, Rohit, *The Science Of Meditation.* Delhi India: Motilal Banarsidas, 1978.

Merton, Thomas, *The Way of Chuang Tzu.* New York: New Directions, 1965.

Molinos, M., *The Spiritual Guide which Disentangles the Soul.* Venice, 1685.

Moss, Richard, *Opening to the Infinite* (Tape 1), Boulder, CO: Sounds True, 1997.

The Mother, *The Supreme Discovery.* Pondicherry, India: Sri Aurobindo Ashram Press, 1992, written 1912.

Narayanananda, S., *The Mysteries of Man, Mind and Mind-Functions*, Fifth Ed., Gylling, Denmark: N. U. Yoga Trust, 1979.

Newell, J. P., *Listening for the Heartbeat of God: A Celtic Spirituality.* New York: Paulist Press, 1997.

Okakura, Kakuzu, *The Book of Tea*. New York: Dover Publications, 1964.

O'Neill, Eugene, *Long Day's Journey into Night*. New Haven: Yale University Press, 1955.

Owadally, Mohamad Y., *Marvellous Bedtime Stories*. Delhi: Rightway Publications, 2003.

Packer, Toni, *The Light of Discovery*. Boston: Charles E. Tuttle Co., 1995.

- *Springwater Center Newsletter*. Springwater Center, 7179 Mill Street, Springwater, New York 14560, October, 1996.

Paramananda, S., *Concentration and Meditation*. Cohasset, MA: Vedanta Center, Eighth Edition, 1982.

Peale, Norman Vincent, *Enthusiasm Makes the Difference*. New York: Fawcett Crest, 1967.

Plotinus, *The Enneads*. In Harvey, 1996, page 135.

Sri Ramakrishna, *Parables of Sri Ramakrishna*. Calcutta: The Indian Press, 1985.

Reps, Paul, *Zen Flesh, Zen Bones: A Collection of Zen and Pre-Zen Writings*. New York: Anchor Books, 1998.

Remen, Rachel Naomi, *Kitchen Table Wisdom*. New York: Riverhead Books, 1996.

- On Defining Spirit, *Noetic Science Review*, 1988, reprinted in Winter, 1998, page 64.

- *The Will to Live and Other Mysteries*, Boulder, CO: Sounds True, 2001.

Robinson, Jonathan (Editor), *The Experience of God.* Carlsbad, CA: Hay House, 1998.

Rubin, Danny, *Groundhog Day.* Columbia Pictures, 1993.

Saraswati, S., *Meditations from the Tantras.* Bihar, India: The Bihar School, 1974.

Stryk, Lucien, Ikemoto, Takashi, *Zen Poems, Prayers, Sermons, Anecdotes, Interviews.* New York: Anchor Books, 1963.

Tanahashi, K., & Schneider, T.D., *Essential Zen.* San Francisco: Harper, 1994, page 21.

Thich Nhat Hanh, *The Miracle of Mindfulness.* Boston: Beacon Press, 1975.

Thoreau, Henry David, *Walden, or Life in the Woods.* New York: The New American Library, 1960.

Tolle, Eckhart, *The Power of Now.* New World Library Audio. Novato, CA, 2001.

-    *Realizing the Power of Now,* Audio Retreat, Boulder, CO: Sounds True, 2007.

Tollifson, Joan, *Bare-Bones Meditation: Waking Up From The Story of My Life.* New York: Bell Tower, 1992.

Untermeyer, Louis (Editor), *Great Poems.* New York: Galahad Books, Simon & Schuster, 1955.

Vaswani, I. L., *Discover Yourself!* Pune, India: Gita Publishing House, undated.

Vivekananda, S., *The Complete Works of Swami Vivekananda.* Calcutta, India: Advaita Ashrama. Second Edition, 1987.

Walker, Susan (Editor), *Speaking of Silence*. New York: Paulist Press, 1987.

Walsh, Roger, An Overview of Research on Meditation. *Noetic Sciences Review*, Spring, 1993, page 36.

Watts, Alan, *This Is It*. New York: Vintage Books, 1958.

- *The Book: On the Taboo Against Knowing Who You Are*. New York: Vintage Books, 1966.

- *Cloud-Hidden, Whereabouts Unknown*. New York: Vintage Books, 1974.

Webster's New World Dictionary, College Edition. New York: The World Publishing Co., 1966.

Weil, Andrew, *Eight Weeks to Optimum Health*. New York: Alfred A. Knopf, 1997.

APPENDIX—EXERCISE INDEX

Alternate Feedback Exercises

Attention Building Exercises

Awareness Exercises

Self-tests

In March, 2009 this book will appear in a new edition titled:
STRAIGHT LINE MEDITATION
Find Focusing Discs and more at www.StraightLineMeditation.com

Contact Master Deac at DeacCataldo@yahoo.com
Contact Carol at CEM1685@aol.com

INDEX

2327344

Made in the USA